A Miscellany for
GARDEN-LOVERS

A Miscellany for
GARDEN-LOVERS

Facts and folklore through the ages

DAVID SQUIRE

green books

Published by
GREEN BOOKS
An imprint of UIT Cambridge Ltd.
www.greenbooks.co.uk

PO Box 145, Cambridge CB4 1GQ, England
+44 (0) 1223 302 041

First published in 2014, in England.

DESIGNER
Glyn Bridgewater

EDITOR
Fiona Corbridge

PICTURE CREDITS
Clipart.com

ISBN 978 0 85784 274 9 (hardback)
ISBN 978 0 85784 275 6 (ePub)
ISBN 978 0 85784 276 3 (pdf)
Also available for Kindle.

10 9 8 7 6 5 4 3 2 1

CONTENTS

For Patricia,
my wife,
who makes all things possible

FOREWORD

Gardening is fun and full of visual, aural and scented rewards. This age-old craft is steeped in mystique, peppered with the handed-down wisdom offered by 'sons of the soil' who grew larger cabbages than their neighbours.

If you think that gardening has become too scientific and wonder where all that hands-on experience has gone, this book mines a rich seam of folkloric advice. You will realize that perhaps those 'oldies' knew a thing or two about growing plants. It is a book for all gardeners, whether experienced or novice, and they can look forward to gaining unexpected tips as well as amusement.

Throughout, this book is packed with historical illustrations that complement the text, giving an insight into gardening subjects from early garden tools to gardening methods, plant and weather folklore, garden gnomes, early lawns, healing plants, life on the farm, and early plant hunters.

You may want to return to a favourite page of the book and for that reason there is a ribbon marker attached to it.

This is a book for all seasons and I wish you well with it.

Sincerely,

David Squire

CHAPTER ONE

Early Garden Tools

Early gardening tools were robust and varied, with many groups of early settlers worldwide developing and refining their own range of equipment. Additionally, tools become specialized to undertake specific garden tasks – for example, for tilling the soil and improving its drainage, or for grafting and pruning. Some tools, especially those used to prune plants and robustly cultivate soil, were developments from types earlier used in warlike situations.

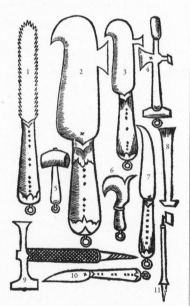

**From Leonard Mascall's
Art of Planting and Grafting, 1572**

SIXTEENTH-CENTURY GRAFTING IMPLEMENTS

Left: 1 Saw; 2 Great knife; 3 Pruning knife; 4 Wimble bit; 5 Mallet; 6 Vine knife; 7 Flifing knife; 8 Grafting chefill; 9 Hammer, file and piercer; 10 Grafting knife; 11 Straffe.

EIGHTEENTH-CENTURY GARDENING IMPLEMENTS

Opposite: 1 Spade; 2 Shovel; 3 Rakes; 4 Rakers (for clearing weeds); 5 Displanter; 6 Pruning knife; 7 Dibbers; 8 Watering can; 9 Beetle; 10 Flower basket; 11 Sieve; 12 Saw; 13 Transplanter; 14 Garden pots; 15 Planer or rabot;

16 Panniers of straw; 17 Mallet; 18 Wheelbarrow; 19 Handbarrow; 20 Caterpillar shears; 21 Garden shears; 22 Double ladder; 23 Pickaxe; 24 Roller; 25 Hook; 26 Glass cloche; 27 Straw bell; 28 Garden fork; 29 Trowel; 30 Hurdle.

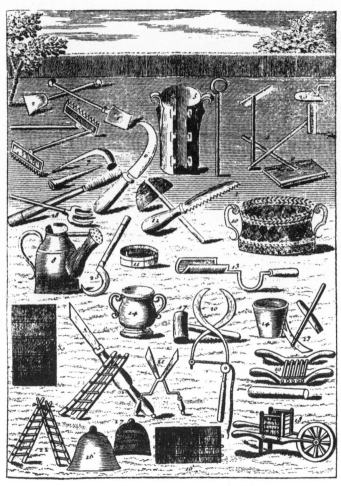

Garden implements from Le Jardinier Fleuriste
by Le Sieur Liger d'Auxerre 1787

MATTOCK

This soil-preparation tool was formed of a stout, round handle and a heavy, spade-like piece of metal set at a right angle to the handle. It was used for turning over and preparing soil, as well as levelling and forming ridges in preparation for crops to be planted.

A mamoty was an Asian derivation, available in several types and primarily used in soil preparation.

EARLY SPADES

Medieval spades were robust and heavy, made of wood and with cutting edges sheathed in metal to make them more durable. The handle was usually T-shaped: a simple and easily constructed design that could be quickly replaced if broken.

Medieval mattock

Medieval spade

ORCHARD TOOLS

Early tools used in orchards were robust and the ones featured opposite (top) are in *A New Orchard and Garden*, published in 1618 by William Lawson (1553–1635). It was printed together with the first horticultural book written solely for women, *The Country Housewife's Garden*.

A New Orchard and Garden, 1618

MAKING HOLES WITH A DIBBER

Dibbers have been used for several hundred years to form a hole into which roots of plants can be inserted, with soil then firmed around them. Sometimes, they were also used when sowing seeds.

Here, a dibber is featured in *The Gardener's Labyrinth*, compiled by Thomas Hill (who probably also wrote under the name Didymus Mountain) and first published in 1577.

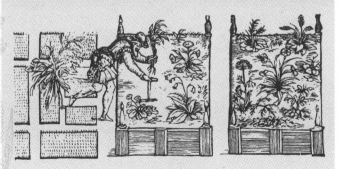

The Gardener's Labyrinth, 1577

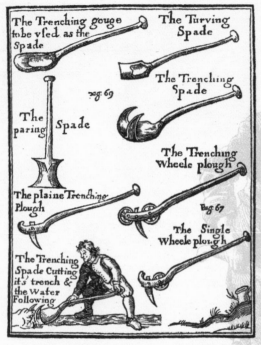

The English Improver Improved, 1649

EARLY ENGLISH FARMING TOOLS

Walter Blith's *The English Improver Improved*, first published in London in 1649, contains a wide range of tools, some for trenching, others for digging, as well as early ploughs.

WHEELBARROW AND HANDBARROW

Wheeled barrows, formed of two handles with a wheel at the other end and able to carry a load, have been used for more than 2,000 years in China and Greece, as seen in agricultural records. In medieval Europe, wheelbarrows appeared sometime between 1170 and 1250, but remained a rarity until the fifteenth century.

Agricultural wheelbarrows of the 1800s were heavy, made of strong wood and often with sides that could be extended upwards to enable larger loads to be carried – but at the risk of the barrow turning over.

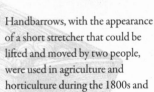

Handbarrows, with the appearance of a short stretcher that could be lifted and moved by two people, were used in agriculture and horticulture during the 1800s and early 1900s. Some were modified with low sides and even given legs so they could be put down more easily.

DAISY FORK AND RAKE

In the late 1800s there appears to have been an obsession with the removal of daisies from lawns, and several types of daisy removers were available. One of these was a daisy fork – it had a notched end for pushing under a daisy, with a handle at the other end for levering the plant out of the ground. Another daisy-removing tool was a daisy rake. This was drawn over a lawn.

FRUIT TREE SQUIRTER

During the 1800s, devices for spraying fruit trees with water were devised to clean both the tree and its fruit. This sprayer, formed of galvanized metal, was featured in the popular weekly gardening magazine *The Gardener's Chronicle* (founded in 1841 and continuing for nearly 150 years) in 1860.

BILLHOOK

The billhook had another life as a weapon of war and during the Middle Ages was frequently made with a sharp curved blade. Additionally, many were fitted with a spear-like head and had spikes added to the back. The English were well known for using these weapons in war and became known as billmen.

In gardens and on farms, billhooks were used to trim and prune trees and hedges. There were many shapes and types of the sharpened metal heads and these varied from country to country. Some billhooks had short handles; others had the head attached to a 1.2–1.8 m (4–8 ft) wooden handle for reaching high branches.

ITALIAN GARDENING TOOLS

This illustration from Pusato's *Giardino di Agricultura*, published in Venice in 1593, details a wide range of agricultural tools.

Billhooks in The Gardener's Labyrinth, 1577

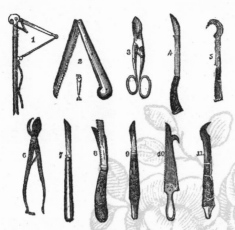

Grafting tools

GRAFTING TOOLS

Nowadays, only a few pruning tools are considered to be necessary, but in earlier times highly specialized ones were used. Here are a few of them:

1 Averruncator – 1.8 m (6 ft) long;
2 Folding pruning handsaw;
3 Bow-slide pruning shears;
4 and 5 Gooseberry pruning knife, straight and hooked blade;
6 Hand-sliding pruning shears;
7 Pruning knife with straight blade and smooth spatula;
8 Pruning knife and saw;
9 Budding knife with ivory spatula;
10 Gentleman's improved pruning saw with billhook;
11 Grafting knife with strong curved blade serving as a chisel, and spatula added to ease open the graft's edges.

TRANSPLANTERS

As well as dibbers and trowels for moving and replanting plants, more ingenious tools were developed in Europe and North America. The transplanters shown here have blades that are opened to enable them to be inserted into the soil around a plant. Counter-pressure then closes the blades around the plant's root ball, so that it can be moved. Some transplanters had the appearance of two garden forks whose tines could be levered together when a plant was being moved.

Transplanters

SYRINGES

During the 1800s, brass syringes became widely available for syringing plants, either with clean water or with chemicals to control pests and diseases. They were strong and rust resistant, with a long life.

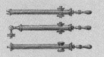

EARLY SECATEURS

Before secateurs, also known as hand pruners, became widely available, knives were used for pruning but needed skill to ensure that the cut was clean and the user escaped unharmed. It is claimed that secateurs were invented in 1815 by the Marquis Bertrand de Moleville, a French aristocrat and politician who had to flee France during the Revolution of 1789. At first they were not popular, but this changed in the late 1800s when the English garden writer William Robinson (1838–1935) promoted their use.

Early secateurs had two blades that crossed each other, with a spring to enable them to open easily after making a cut.

VINEYARD BIRD SCARER

Birds, and especially starlings, cause a great deal of damage to plants and fruits. During the sixteenth century, the *klopotec* (sometimes *klapotetz*) was developed in wine-growing areas of Slovenia, Austria and Croatia. In Germany it was called the *Windradi* or *Windmühle*, while in England it became known as the wind-rattle or wind-clapper.

It was formed of several blades driving an axle that rotated and activated wooden hammers to produce a sharp rattling noise. The whole device was mounted on a high, strong pole.

GARDEN AND ORCHARD LADDERS

Ladders were invariably needed to enable high hedges to be trimmed, as well as for pruning fruit trees and harvesting their fruits. Those made for use when clipping hedges often had a small platform at the top, while orchard ladders were invariably constructed with three legs (two with rungs between them and the other to give support when extended). This design was cheap to construct and enabled the pruner or picker to get close to the tree and the fruits. Apples needed to be picked individually and with care to prevent them from getting bruised, as this made them impossible to store.

POLED WATERING CAN

In the middle to late nineteenth century, the Victorians' love of gadgets led to the invention of many new tools and devices. These included a watering can fitted into a bracket mounted at the top of a 1.5 m (5 ft) bamboo cane. The can was operated by pulling on a strong piece of string.

CHAPTER TWO

Inverting the Sod

Traditionally, sons of the soil would dig the soil with a spade in autumn and winter to improve its structure, killing annual weeds, exposing soil pests to frost and birds, and improving surface drainage. They would also mix in decomposed farmyard manure and vegetable waste from kitchens and gardens. It was hard work, especially if the soil was heavy and contained a large proportion of clay. But it was – and still is – a necessary part of gardening.

Every Man His Own Gardener, 1767

GARDEN WRITER

John Abercrombie (1726–1806) was a well-known disseminator of gardening information and in 1767 co-authored with Thomas Mawe *Every Man His Own Gardener*. The book went into several editions and this illustration was the frontispiece in one of them, made when he was 72.

As a young man, Abercrombie worked at the Royal Gardens, Kew, and later taught botany at the University of Cambridge. In later years he set up a successful market gardening business in North London. Also, he wrote many further gardening books and became known as 'the great teacher of gardening'.

Evolution of digging tools

SINGLE DIGGING

The most popular and easiest method of digging is to dig to a depth of a spade's blade – about 27 cm (11 in.), known as a 'spit'. An initial trench is taken out across one end of the plot, and soil from the next trench to be dug is systematically inverted into it. Perennial weeds are removed, but annual types are put into the base of the trench, together with well-decomposed manure and vegetable waste.

Gardener, 1850

DOUBLE DIGGING

This involves digging the soil to a depth of about 60 cm (2 ft). Initially, a trench about 30 cm (12 in.) deep and 60 cm (2 ft) wide is taken out across one end of the plot that is to be dug.

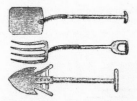

A garden fork is used to turn over soil in the base (the lower 'spit') to break it up. Soil from the next 60 cm (2 ft), adjacent to the first trench, is then turned into the trench and the soil in the base turned over by using a garden fork. The sequence is repeated until the plot is completely dug.

BASTARD TRENCHING

As its name implies, this is heavy, tiring work but sometimes necessary when endeavouring to break up an impervious layer low in the soil that prevents water draining from the surface and roots extending deep into the soil.

It involves progressively working down a plot of soil, digging it out to a depth of about 60 cm (2 ft) – keeping the topsoil separate from the lower 'spit' – and then using a garden fork to turn over soil in the trench's base to a further depth of about 27 cm (11 in.). Soil is then returned to the trench, first the subsoil, then the topsoil.

RIDGING

This is a way of digging land to leave an increased surface area open to the winter weathering effects of frost, rain and wind. It breaks down its surface and produces finer soil in spring, which assists in the sowing of seeds. Additionally, on slopes it enables excess rainwater to run off the land more freely. Light soils, with a high sand content, do not require ridging but where there is a high proportion of clay this is an ideal way to improve it.

Initially a wide trench, 30 cm (1 ft) deep, is taken out across the upper end of the plot which is to be dug. The land is then systematically dug, creating ridges by using soil from a series of three spadefuls to form them. In spring – before sowing seeds or planting crops – it is necessary to rake the area level.

Digging and manuring, early eighteenth century

MANURING

The above early eighteenth-century illustration shows gardeners manuring the land, spreading the manure and then using a spade to dig it in. Animal dung, from horse manure to pigeon droppings, was decomposed with straw and then dug into the soil to improve its structure and provide growth nutrients for plants.

In earlier times, China and some other countries, including Korea, widely used human excrement as a fertilizer in regions where animal manure was not available or in limited supply.

SWEET PEA TRENCHES

In addition to methods of deeply cultivating soil, such as double digging and bastard trenching, the land for a few specific crops needed to be specially prepared – and none more so than for exhibition sweet peas. The soil was dug in autumn to three 'spits' deep, the broad trenches then left open to the weathering effect of rain, frost and wind and, in spring, soil was gradually replaced in them, ready for early summer planting.

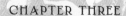
CHAPTER THREE

Draining Soil

Keeping land drained but able to retain sufficient moisture for the growth of plants has been the desire of farmers and gardeners for thousands years. The Romans knew about land drainage and moisture conservation, with Pliny the Elder, Lucius Junius Moderatus Columella and Cato the Elder writing about farm management some two millennia ago. Since then, with the increasing need to bring larger amounts of land throughout the world into food production, the imperative to drain land has not gone away.

DRAINING FENLAND

Fens are large, low-lying and marshy areas that need different drainage techniques from established agricultural land. It was not until the 1630s that there was effective drainage for the Fens in Norfolk, England. Large channels were cut, and pumps (first powered by wind, then steam; later, diesel and electricity) removed excess water. Unfortunately, the peat-based land has shrunk, leaving large areas below the high tide sea level.

Cross-section of drainage trench

EARLY LAND-DRAINING TOOLS

The creation of trenches in which pipe drains could be laid was usually done with an ordinary spade. However, in heavy clay soil, a range of narrow-bladed spades and scoops were used.

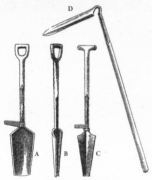

Drainage trench tools

In the illustration above, spade 'A' was used to dig out soil from the upper part of a trench; it had a piece of stout metal secured at a right angle to the shaft for pressing the blade into the soil. Spades 'B' and 'C' are narrower and were good for digging soil from the base of a trench. In addition, tool 'D' enabled loose soil in the bottom of the trench to be easily removed.

Drainage trenches were formed to have a slight slope, with the end reaching a drainage sump (filled with coarse rubble) or just channelled into a ditch or stream. The illustration above left shows a drainage pipe laid directly on soil in the base of a trench. Nowadays, however, it is recommended that you have a layer of gravel for the pipe to rest upon, 7.5–10 cm (3–4 in.) thick, with a similarly thick layer of gravel above. Soil is then placed over the gravel and allowed to settle.

THE NEED TO DRAIN LAND

Continually wet soil is cold and slow to warm up in spring, a season when many seeds are sown and plants put into the ground. Additionally, continually wet land is unworkable and if trodden upon, this consolidates it and further impairs drainage. Continually wet land also tends to be acidic, which encourages roots to decay.

CONTOUR PLOUGHING

Contour ploughing (or contour farming) was practised in ancient times by the Phoenicians (1200–539 BC) in Canaan, which covered most of the western and coastal part of the Fertile Crescent, where the birth of agriculture partly began some 10,000 years ago. Contour ploughing is the practice of ploughing across a slope, following its elevation, to control water run-off and possible soil erosion.

In contour ploughing, the cutting edge formed by a plough's blade has to be vertical, rather than at a right angle to the slope. This causes the flow of water running down the slope to slow, giving it more time to be absorbed by the soil.

This ploughing technique is used in many countries. In some areas of North America, it has reduced the loss of soil by 65 per cent.

Illustration from Spring Plowing by Charles Malam, 1928

HIGH RAINFALL PROBLEMS

In countries where there is a high rainfall, it is usually cheaper and better to have ditches alongside flat cultivated land, rather than installing drains. However, such trenches are vital on steep land in tropical and subtropical regions where soil erosion is a problem.

On steep, unterraced and undrained land up to 42 tonnes of topsoil per hectare (17 tons per acre) can be lost every year. This loss of precious topsoil clogs channels, often causing flooding in low-lying areas many kilometres away.

BRUSHWOOD, STONE AND GRAVEL DRAINS

Early and simple drainage systems were created by digging trenches that ran into in a stream or dyke. The trenches were partly filled with brushwood (mostly ash), stones, gravel or large shells. Such drains had a limited life as, eventually, surface soil washed into them, causing clogging.

TILE DRAINS

Although two Romans, Pliny the Elder and Cato the Elder, described using tile drains to remove excessive water from land, the technique of using a form of clay tile did not gain prominence in Britain until towards the 1700s. At first, this involved cutting a small, rectangular channel in the base of a trench and putting a roofing tile over it. Another way was to lay two hollowed-out bricks face to face, so that the hollow formed a pipe. A later improvement was to

Illustration from Spring Plowing by Charles Malam, 1928

Pliny the Elder

turn over the edges of a roofing tile into a horseshoe shape before firing, to give rigidity.

DRAINAGE ENCOURAGED

An English statute of 1826 (confirmed in 1839 and 1840) exempted land drains from the duty normally paid on bricks. But they had to be solely for draining the land and stamped with the word 'drain'.

EARLY PIPE DRAINS

In the late eighteenth and early nineteenth centuries, drainage pipes were expensive because they were individually shaped by hand around a drum. A machine to make them was invented in the mid-nineteenth century, resulting in the pipes becoming increasingly available to farmers.

These early pipe drains had a bore of about 2.5 cm (1 in.), but later more practical ones – first 5 cm (2 in.) and then 7.5 cm (3 in.) – became available.

Large areas of land were drained in this way up to the 1890s but, with the continuing agricultural depression, the practical and financial benefit was lost. However, during the 1930s, with the introduction of tile-laying machines, the practice was renewed. Later, this was replaced by mole drainage, which was cheaper but did not have such a long life.

MOLE DRAINAGE

This drainage method is still used today. A projectile-shaped iron known as a mole, usually 6–8 cm (2½–3 in.) in diameter, is dragged through the soil at depths of 38–75 cm (15–30 in.). The mole is attached to a strong, knife-edged, soil-cutting coulter, which is secured through wires to a power source. (This was initially a steam traction engine positioned on the headland of the field being drained. Tracked tractors later came into use.)

Where shallow mole drainage is performed, the mole-like tunnels are 1.8–2.7 m (6–9 ft) apart, but when installed at deeper depths they are 2.7–3.6 m (9–12 ft) apart.

CHAPTER FOUR

Conserving Moisture in Soil

Keeping soil evenly moist, but not waterlogged, has been the aim of those working the land for thousands of years. Both air and moisture in the soil are essential for the growth of roots and development of stems and leafy growth, but it is a difficult balance to maintain throughout the year. However, many ingenious methods of conserving soil moisture, as well as of applying water, have been used.

STONE MULCHES

The Romans knew the value of stone mulches to prevent soil erosion, retain moisture in the soil and to keep the land cool in summer. A stone mulch also prevented heavy summer rain from contacting bare soil and then splashing on to plants.

Both Lucius Junius Moderatus Columella in the first century AD and Virgil (Pubilus Vergillus Maro) in the last century BC advocated this technique, especially around grapes and apricots. And, of course, the technique of covering soil around alpine plants with shingle is now well known.

SOIL MULCHING

Regularly hoeing the soil's surface (sometimes known as 'natural mulching') during summer kills weeds, which rob soil of moisture and nutrients. Additionally, it breaks up the surface soil and prevents water rising by capillary action and escaping into the atmosphere.

Medieval agricultural worker

LIVING MULCHES

In agriculture, these are under-sown or interplanted with a main crop and intended to act as a mulch, suppressing weeds, regulating the soil's temperature, and protecting against erosion by water and wind. As a technique, a living mulch is relatively recent and the outcome of research, mainly in North America, in the 1970s.

Some ground-covering plants, such as clovers and vetches, have the ability to 'fix' nitrogen present in the air and add it to the soil. This reduces the need for nitrogenous fertilizers to be applied to the land.

29

DECAYED GARDEN COMPOST

As well as reducing moisture loss from soil, keeping the land cool, preventing erosion and suppressing weed growth, a mulch of well-decayed manure or compost provides plants with food. In earlier centuries, before the advent of the motor car, horse manure was in bountiful supply and particularly valued. Nowadays, well-rotted farmyard manure is used, together with composted vegetable waste.

DRY FARMING

This is an agricultural technique dating back to about 1870 and used on crops such as winter wheat growing on non-irrigated land with little rainfall. It relies on the moisture-conserving tillage of the soil and drought-resistant crops. It is practised on the Great Plains of North America, and in the Middle East, Argentina, Australia and the steppes of Eurasia. It has also been used in the Granada region of Spain.

WATERING WITH A SHADUF

The shaduf (or shadoof) was originally developed in ancient Mesopotamia some 2,000 years ago, later becoming widely used in Egypt. It is still employed in areas of Africa and Asia to raise water from a river or stream and to place it in irrigation channels on the land. A counterbalance allows it to raise water effortlessly, and it is able to lift more than 2,500 litres (660 gallons) in a day.

THE PERSIAN WHEEL

The Persian wheel or rahat was a system for raising water, still in use in some countries today, formed of a chain of buckets secured around a wheel. It was turned by a system of cogs and interlocking wheels and usually powered by a pair of oxen who walked in a circle.

IRRIGATION IN THE SAHARA AND INDIA

In these hot areas, where water is often found deep in the ground, skin bags were lowered over a pulley, with bullocks, donkeys, camels or slaves used to raise the water. In this way, water was often lifted 30–60 m (100–200 ft). The water was used for drinking purposes and watering crops.

ARCHIMEDEAN INFLUENCE

The Greek mathematician, physicist, engineer, inventor and astronomer Archimedes of Syracuse (287–212 BC) invented the screw pump. Basically, it was a screw-shaped blade inside a cylinder and, it is claimed, was originally designed to raise and remove bilge water from ships. It was later employed to raise water into irrigation channels.

NEW WORLD IRRIGATION

In the dry Pueblo regions of Arizona, ancient irrigation ditches can be traced. In Peru and Mexico, these were highly sophisticated and extensive, clinging to the sides of mountains as well as passing through tunnels. Some of the irrigation canals are said to have been 800 km (500 miles) long.

WINDMILLS AND PUMPS

Windmills were used to raise water from wells and rivers in about AD 1200, several centuries before they were employed to grind corn. Canvas sails were fitted vertically and with gearing, a shaft used to power a water-lifting device.

By the 1500s, double-action pumps (earlier devised by the Romans) were in use in Europe. These were able to lift water on both the push and pull strokes. Simple single-action pumps, with one end placed in a barrel of water, were used to water gardens towards the end of that century, as illustrated in *The Gardener's Labyrinth* by Thomas Hill (1577). This is said to be the first popular gardening book to appear in the English language.

Pumps were also used to lift water from rivers and canals into networks of irrigation channels between flower beds. Care was needed, however, not to disturb and wash away the soil.

Watering, from The Gardener's Labyrinth, 1577

EARLY WATERING CANS

By the early 1600s, primitive watering pots had acquired handles and become both ornate and functional.

This led, through earthenware jugs with perforated spouts, to the metal watering cans of the eighteenth century.

SUNKEN BEDS

In hot countries with a low rainfall, the creation of sunken beds (sometimes known as 'basin' gardening) to grow plants in has been known for several centuries as a way to conserve soil moisture. The beds are dug out and the subsoil removed and replaced with topsoil mixed with organic material such as well-decayed farmyard manure or vegetable compost. The surface is allowed to settle below the surrounding soil and the entire bed well watered before being planted.

CHAPTER FIVE

Sowing Seeds

Seeds represent the seasonal start to many garden and farm crops, an introduction to new life and part of the cycle of plant life. Whether sown in a garden or on a farm, seeds need air, warmth and moisture to encourage germination. Some are able to germinate in either light or darkness; a few will only start their growth processes when in darkness. However, they all need a firm base in which roots can develop to support the resultant plants.

Hans Schönsperger's Augsburger Kalender, 1487

SOWING SEEDS

The art of sowing seeds evenly by hand is an age-old craft and one that takes many years to perfect. A mechanical way of 'broadcasting' seed was developed in 1780 in the form of a small hopper, cradled around the neck and held at waist height; it fed seeds into a geared mechanical device which then scattered them. However the English agricultural pioneer Jethro

Eighteenth-century engraving

Tull (1674–1741) had, in 1701, perfected a horse-drawn seed drill that economically sowed seeds in neat rows.

MOUSE-PROOFING SEEDS

In the nineteenth and early twentieth centuries, seeds were often moistened with paraffin before being sown to deter mice from eating them.

SPECIALIZED SEED SOWER

In the early to mid-1800s, one mechanism for sowing turnip and mangold seeds on ridges involved arched rollers that consolidated loose soil and then dribbled seeds along the top.

SOWING MAIZE

Native Americans showed early settlers a way of sowing maize that became known as the 'Indian' method. This involved forming a flat-topped mound, about 30 cm (12 in.) high and 50 cm (20 in.) wide, in which rotten fish and eels had been buried. In each mound, four or five seeds were spaced about 15 cm (6 in.) apart and 2.5 cm (1 in.) deep. It was essential to sow the seeds after all risk of frost had passed.

MECHANICAL MAIZE SOWING

In North America, mechanical ways to sow maize seeds in drills included a 'two-row maize planter' drawn by a horse. Early models involved a shoe-type furrow-opener, while later ones had a rotary disc that more easily opened up a drill to an even depth without excessively disturbing the surrounding soil.

THE INFLUENCE OF THE MOON

In country areas during the eighteenth century there were various and often contradictory recommendations about sowing seeds and the influence of the moon on germination and growth. One claimed that seeds should be sown when the moon was waxing (increasing in size) in order to germinate most readily. Another advised sowing during the new moon; yet another in the last few days of the wane.

One popular saying was:

Sow peas (good Trull),
The moon past full,
Fine seeds then sow,
Whilst the moon doth grow.

And another:

Sow peasen and beans in the wane of the moon,
Who soweth them sooner, he soweth too soon,
That they with the planet may rest and arise,
And flourish with bearing most plentiful wise.

There are some gardeners who still sow seeds according to the position of the moon.

French, eighteenth century

RELIGIOUS GUIDANCE

Even until late in the nineteenth century, sowing guidance was taken from the clergy, with the saying:

> *When the parson begins to read Genesis, it's time to sow black oats.*

DEATH PREDICTION

As a way to concentrate a seed-sower's mind when sowing seeds, there were several well-known superstitions in Europe and North America. Should a sower make a mistake and fail to sow seeds in a drill, it was said that someone connected with the farm would die before reaping time arrived. Even in the late 1930s there was a belief in Britain that:

> *Mustn't miss a row, or we'll lose one of the family.*

Matthew 13:4 – the sower

PROTECTING SEEDS

Seeds are vulnerable to wet and dry
variations in the weather, as well as
to birds. A traditional sower's rule
advised:

One to rot and one to grow,
one for the pigeon
and one for the crow.

Additionally, young boys were enrolled
to run around the field with clappers,
shouting:

Away, away, away birds,
Take a little bit and come another
day, birds.
Great birds, little birds, pigeons
and crows,
I'll up with my clapper and down
she goes.

Another rhyme was:

One for the rook, one for the crow,
One to die and one to grow,
Plant your seeds in a row.

And:

One for pheasant, one for crow,
One to eat and one to grow.

BIRD CLAPPER

An early way to discourage birds
was with a bird clapper. This had
a central piece of wood (similar
to the head of a tennis racket, but
smaller) with a handle, and two
pieces of wood secured on either
side. As the clapper was waved,
one of the pieces of wood clapped
against the central part, making a
sharp and unexpected noise.

TESTING FOR SOIL WARMTH

A traditional way to assess a soil's
temperature and suitability for
sowing seeds was for a farmer
to take his trousers off and sit
on bare soil. If it resulted in a
temperature shock, sowing was
delayed. Another, and perhaps more
practical warmth-testing method
was for the sower to place a bare
elbow on the ground; if the soil felt
warm, sowing could proceed.

PROTECTING CARROT SEED

To protect carrots from carrot fly, the soil was sprinkled with crushed mothballs which were then shallowly hoed into the soil.

POTATO PLANTING RHYME

Potato tubers (sometimes known as 'seeds') were traditionally planted on Maundy Thursday (also known as Holy Thursday, a variable occasion between 19th March and 22nd April).

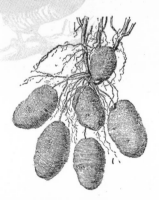

Also, a traditional Scottish rhyme gave guidance about planting:

When you hear the cuckoo shout,
'Tis time to plant your tatties out.

SWEET PEA GUIDANCE

For large and fragrant flowers, sweet peas were traditionally sown on St Patrick's Day (17th March). Guidance on plant supports suggested that you should never use wood cut from an ash tree as it made plants recoil if it touched them.

A HAIRCUT HELPS!

Beans grow best in nitrogen-rich soil and in the 1800s, trenches for planting included hair trimmings gathered from local hairdressers, as well as horsehair extracted from old mattresses.

CHAPTER SIX

Early Plant Hunters

The desire to search for native plants growing in other countries and to bring them back to grow in gardens has long been felt by gardeners. The earliest plant-hunting expedition was probably the one initiated by Queen Hatshepsut of Egypt in 1495 BC, when she sent plant hunters to the Land of Punt (Somalia) to obtain living specimens of trees whose fragrant resin yielded frankincense.

A PERILOUS OCCUPATION

Searching for new plants was a passion for the Scot David Douglas (1799–1834) who, having worked in the Glasgow Botanic Garden, was sent to search for plants in North America in 1823 by the Royal Horticultural Society. He explored British Columbia and Oregon, discovering many conifers as well as the flowering currant (*Ribes*), red-barked dogwood (*Cornus alba*), Oregon grape (*Mahonia aquifolium*) and *Lupinus polyphyllus*, the ancestor of most garden lupins.

David Douglas

Tragically, he died in 1834 in the Sandwich Islands (later known as Hawaii) after falling into a pit-trap dug by islanders to catch wild cattle, which already held a bull. His body was removed by two islanders and an Englishman, Ned; Douglas's faithful dog was close by. He was taken to the British consul's house at Wahoo, and buried there.

Lupinus polyphyllus

Wardian case

THE WARDIAN CASE

In 1829, the London doctor Nathaniel Bagshaw Ward accidentally discovered that plants could be grown in enclosed environments and invented the Wardian case. Many people began to grow small ornamental plants in Wardian cases as a hobby. Additionally, the cases enabled plants to be transported over vast distances and through hostile climates.

DANGEROUS INSECTS

Though plants from northern and southern Africa were easily collected, equatorial Africa presented greater difficulties. The malaria-carrying mosquito gravely endangered the health of Europeans.

Plant-hunting in the region of the Louisiana Purchase in North America, as well as settlements in the Dutch East Indies, was curtailed by mosquitoes until the early 1900s, when chemicals became available to control or deter them.

Hibiscus rosa-sinensis

ASIAN GEM

One of the most beautiful plants to come from tropical Asia and China is *Hibiscus rosa-sinensis*, locally known as the blacking plant because juice in the flowers was used by women to blacken their eyebrows and hair, as well as shoes.

PROTECTION AGAINST RATS

In the beautiful north-eastern Indian state of Nagaland, there grows a herb with fruits that remain gummy for several years. These fruits were placed in strategic positions in granary huts, and when rats attempted to push past them, their eyelids became glued.

William Bligh

LEGENDARY MUTINY

In 1787 a directive given by the British Admiralty to Commanding Lieutenant William Bligh resulted in him sailing to Tahiti (then known as Otaheite) in the Pacific Ocean in the HMS *Bounty*, to load breadfruit (*Artocarpus altilis*) plants for transfer to the West Indies. The plan was to see if breadfruit would grow well there and become a cheap source of food for slaves. On the return voyage, and when laden with plants, a famous mutiny occurred on 28th April 1789, led by Fletcher Christian. Unfortunately, this has obscured the purpose of the voyage.

This botanical experiment had been proposed by Sir Joseph Banks who, at that time, was the unofficial director of Kew Gardens, England. Banks had been the botanist on board Lieutenant James Cook's ship, the HMS *Bark Endeavour*, when it visited Tahiti during Cook's first voyage (1768–71) to observe, in 1769, the transit of Venus and to seek evidence of the postulated Terra Australis Incognita (unknown southern land). From his activities during this southern voyage, Banks is credited with the initial introduction to the Western world of species of acacia, mimosa and eucalyptus.

Artocarpus altilis

As a postscript to the mutiny on HMS *Bounty*, Bligh (now captain) led a second expedition to Tahiti to collect breadfruit. This he did and took them to the West Indies, but the slaves on Jamaica refused to eat them.

MEDICINAL TEA

The evergreen creeping shrub *Gaultheria procumbens*, native to eastern North America, was introduced into Europe by 1762. It proved to be as invaluable to early settlers as it was to Native Americans and indigenous animals, including the wild turkey, grouse, pheasant and red fox.

Gaultheria procumbens

The low-growing *Gaultheria procumbens* is a plant with many common names, including wintergreen, checkerberry, tea berry and mountain tea. Native Americans brewed a tea from the leaves to alleviate aches and pains, headaches, sore throats and rheumatism. Early European settlers ate the berries in pies, while distillation of the leaves produced wintergreen oil, used as an antiseptic and to treat rheumatism and lumbago.

PARSON'S SORE THROAT

We owe the discovery and introduction of *Heliotropium peruvianum* (now *H. arborescens*), popularly known as cherry pie, to the French naturalist and mathematician Charles-Marie de la Condamine (1701–74). When in Peru and in the Valley of the Cordilleras, he found this highly fragrant plant. Seeds entered Europe by way of France and the plant was said to cure warts. But its main use was as an astringent in throat pastilles, and it was claimed that these cured 'clergyman's sore throat'.

THE LAND OF FIRE

Few plants create such a blaze of colour as the Californian poppy, *Eschscholzia californica*. It set its native country, California, so alive with colour that the Spaniards called the region 'The Land of Fire'. It was discovered by Scottish surgeon and botanist Archibald Menzies in 1792. Although then raised at Kew, the plant became lost. In 1815 it was rediscovered by the French botanist Louis Charles Adélaïde de Chamissot on a scientific voyage around the world, and named after a fellow voyager, the Russian botanist Dr Johann Friedrich Eschscholz.

Native Americans ate the leaves, used the pollen cosmetically and employed the seeds in cookery. In 1903 it became the official state flower of California.

Eschscholzia californica

CONFUSING NAMES

Both the African marigold (*Tagetes erecta*) and French marigold (*Tagetes patula*) are natives of Mexico but arrived separately in Europe. The larger species, *Tagetes erecta*, arrived in Spain in the sixteenth century and became popular in southern Europe under the name 'rose of the Indies'. By about 1535 it had become established in North Africa, considered to be a locally native flower and reintroduced into Europe as *Flos Africanus*; it arrived in England by 1568 and became known as the African marigold.

The French marigold (*Tagetes patula*) probably arrived in Europe by the same route as the African type. Because it was smaller and less flamboyant, it became known derisorily as the 'common Africane'. It is said to have been introduced into Britain by Huguenot refugees after the St Bartholomew's Day Massacre in 1572.

Tagetes erecta

Tagetes patula

TURBANED BEAUTY

Few bulbous plants are as impressive as the crown imperial (*Fritillaria imperialis*), native to a wide area from Anatolia across the plateau of Iran to Afghanistan, Pakistan and the Himalayan foothills. It was introduced to Vienna by the Flemish doctor Jules Charles de L'Ecluse (often known as Carolus Clusius) in 1576 and known as the Persian lily.

He had a botanical role at the Imperial Gardens in Vienna and through contacts in the Turkish court at Constantinople received seeds and bulbs from Western Asia.

This plant was admired by the Emperor Jahangir, ruler of the Mughal empire from 1606 until his death in 1627, and its image was carved into the walls of the Taj Mahal at Agra, India on the instructions of his successor, his son Prince Khurram (1592–1666), who took the title of Shah Jehan.

Taj Mahal

DAZZLING DAHLIAS

The brightly coloured, frost-tender dahlia comes from Mexico, where it must have been grown in Aztec gardens for hundreds of years, because at the time of the Spanish conquest (1519–24), some types of cultivated dahlia were not known in the wild.

The first European to describe dahlias was Francisco Hernández de Toledo (1514–78), botanist and physician to Philip of Spain. In 1789, Vincent Cervantes of the botanic gardens in Mexico City sent seeds to the Royal Gardens at Madrid, and the first ones to germinate and bloom produced semi-double flowers; they were named *Dahlia pinnata* in honour of Dr Dahl, a Swedish botanist and pupil of Linnaeus.

Plants sent to Kew Gardens, England, failed to establish themselves, probably as a result of their needs being unknown. However, later ones sent to Kew in 1804 germinated and produced seeds. Additionally, the Empress Josephine grew dahlias (it is claimed she planted the first tubers herself) in her garden at Malmaison, near Paris. At the end of the Napoleonic Wars in 1815, many French varieties were imported into Britain and by 1829 the dahlia was a fashionable flower throughout Europe.

Dahlia

Kew Gardens

47

Anemone hupehensis

SPREAD OF THE TEA TRADE

At the end of the First Opium War (1839–42) between the British and Chinese, Hong Kong and Southern Kowloon was ceded to the British and other port entries opened up. In the late winter of 1843, Robert Fortune (1812–80) was sent out by the Horticultural Society (later Royal Horticultural Society) to China to seek plants. He subsequently made other expeditions to China, collecting 190 species or varieties of plants including the Japanese anemone (*Anemone hupehensis*), bleeding heart (*Dicentra spectablis*), azaleas, viburnums, camellias, forsythia and weigela. But, commercially, his fame is for introducing the tea plant to India, so breaking the Chinese monopoly.

Dicentra Spectabilis

CALAMITIES OF TRAVEL

In 1824, Dr Thomas Coulter (1793–1843), an Irish physician, botanist and explorer, arrived in Vera Cruz, eastern Mexico. Initially he was occupied as a land surveyor. Later, after being waylaid by bandits, encountering a shipwreck and an outbreak of cholera, he eventually managed to get about 50,000 plant specimens from Mexico to London. Tragically, however, a box containing his journals and botanical notes was totally lost between London and Dublin!

His 'finds' include the beautiful Californian tree poppy (*Romneya coulteri*) native to California and Mexico.

PLANT HUNTING IN NORTH AMERICA

In the western states of North America, the hunt for plants began much later than on the country's eastern side. Some areas, especially Alaska, had been explored by Russians and plants taken to the botanic garden in St Petersburg. But it was not until 1804 (after the Louisiana Purchase in 1803) that army captains Meriwether Lewis and William Clark began the first transcontinental exploration of the continent.

They set off from St Louis, crossed the continent and in 1805 reached the Columbia River, on the borders of what are now the states of Oregon and Washington, then travelling down to the Pacific coast. They sent back many plants and on the return journey collected seeds of the Oregon grape (*Mahonia aquifolium*) and snowberry (*Symphoricarpos racemosus*, now *S. albus*). They gathered many now popular garden plants, including the blanket flower (*Gaillardia aristata*), avalanche lily (*Erythronium grandiflorum*) and creambush (*Holodiscus discolor*).

William Clark

Gaillardia aristata

Mahonia aquifolium

SOUTH AMERICAN DISCOVERIES

In about 1840, the famous Veitch plant nursery, based in Exeter and London, sent Cornishman William Lobb (1809–64) to South America. He arrived in Rio and travelled across the country to Chile. He returned home but was soon sailing to South America again, where he discovered an immense range of plants, including Darwin's berberis (*Berberis darwinii*), flame creeper (*Tropaeolum speciosum*), Chilean bellflower (*Lapageria rosea*) and taique (*Desfontainia spinosa*).

Desfontainia spinosa

THE FAMED CHRYSANTHEMUM

Few flowers are better known than chrysanthemums, which can be traced back to 500 BC and have now travelled in various forms to most parts of the world. Early types were yellow, while in the Tang Dynasty in China, AD 618–907, white-flowered forms were known.

Chrysanthemum,
Japanese painting

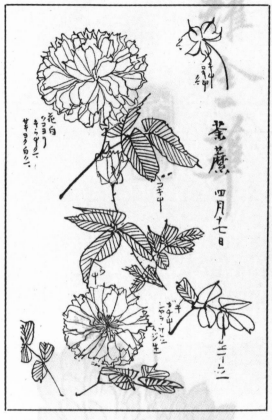

Chrysanthemum, Japanese painting

Chrysanthemums became closely associated with Japan and in 1797 were adopted as the personal emblem of the emperor, later appearing on the Japanese flag as sixteen petals around a central disc. This image is often considered to be the rising sun; on the modern flag it has been simplified to a disc.

During 1688, chrysanthemums were recorded in Holland and in the Chelsea Physic Garden, London, in 1764. Between 1820 and 1830, nearly 70 varieties were introduced and the first English flower show where chrysanthemums were displayed was held in 1843.

CHAPTER SEVEN

Plant Folklore

Plants have become woven into all parts of our lives. Many are grown for their food value, others for the beauty of their leaves or flowers, while some are notorious for their poisonous nature. Many are famed for their medicinal qualities; some were used to cloak incipient decay in food in earlier times. And a surprising number of them are steeped in plant folklore.

Crocus sativus

DANGEROUS LAUGHTER

The saffron crocus (*Crocus sativus*), native to Mediterranean regions, has long been acclaimed for the saffron derived from its dried stigmas (female reproductive parts). These have been used as a condiment, medicament, disinfectant and dye. But just as interesting is its supposed power to provoke mirth and merriment; unfortunately, it is claimed that an overdose could cause dangerously uncontrolled laughter – and loss of life!

DEADLY OLEANDER

The oleander or rose bay (*Nerium oleander*) is often grown as a houseplant in temperate countries, but in Mediterranean regions it develops into an evergreen shrub 3 m (10 ft) or more high. All parts are extremely poisonous. During the wars (early 1800s) fought for control of the Iberian Peninsula, French soldiers used oleander wood as skewers when cooking meat; sadly, several of them died.

Nerium oleander

Mandragors officinarum

DEMONIC MANDRAKE

The mandrake (*Mandragora officinarum* and earlier *Atropa mandragora*) is steeped in folklore. It was said to grow under the gallows of murderers. If pulled from the soil it would shriek, and those who heard it would die. To avoid this, a dog was tethered to the plant, so that when tempted by food just out of its reach it pulled it from the ground, risking death itself.

The plant is native to northern Italy and the western Balkans, and was used as an anaesthetic some 3,000 years ago. Before an operation or the removal of a tooth, a dried anodyne of mandragora and camphor was reconstituted in boiling water and a steaming sponge held over the patient's nostrils until he was unconscious. Later, by the end of the eighth century, Anglo-Saxon doctors (often known as 'leeches') were using this plant as a painkiller.

It was also claimed that the plant had medicinal qualities, including the ability to ease rheumatism and heal ulcers.

SHAKESPEAREAN MANDRAKE

The English playwright William Shakespeare (1564–1616) knew the nature of mandrake and mentions it in several of his plays.

In *Othello* he writes:

Not poppy, nor mandragora,
Nor all the drowsy syrups of the world,
Shall ever medicine thee
to that sweet sleep,
Which thou owedst yesterday.

And in *Romeo and Juliet*:

Shrieks like mandrakes
torn out of the earth.

A LOVER'S DELIGHT

Reseda odorata

Mignonette (*Reseda odorata*), native to Egypt, has achieved fame through the claim that good fortune follows a lover who rolls three times in a bed of mignonette!

KISSING RHYMES

Perhaps one of the most popular pieces of folklore about gorse (*Ulex europaeus*) is revealed in the saying: 'When gorse is out of bloom, kissing's out of season.' Happily, gorse flowers all year, with an abundance of bright yellow, pea-shaped, honey-and-almond-scented flowers.

LIVING IN CLOVER

A four-leaf clover brings more than immediate good luck; young men and women who find one are said to meet their future love on the same day.

An old country rhyme describing a four-leaf clover suggests:

One leaf for fame,
And one for wealth,
And one for a faithful lover,
And one to bring you glorious health,
Are all in a four-leaf clover.

Embrace, woodcut, Clare Leighton (1898–1989)

FORETELLING A HUSBAND

At one time, girls would throw an apple paring over a shoulder in the hope that it would fall on the floor in the shape of a lover's initials.

OMENS OF LOVE AND MARRIAGE

Myrtle flowers were once used in bridal bouquets and sprigs taken from them were inserted in soil near the bride's new home (bridesmaids usually undertook this task as it was thought to be unlucky for a bride to do it). However, should the sprig not develop roots, it was taken to be an indication that the bridesmaid would not marry.

CATCHING A HUSBAND!

Customs rooted in folklore have frequently been used by maidens to foretell and entrap a husband. One calls for a girl to walk through a garden or churchyard on Midsummer's Eve and throw hempseed over her shoulder, chanting:

Hempseed I set, hempseed I sow,
The man that is my true love,
Come after me and mow.

And behind her, it is claimed, would come an image of her future husband.

Cannabis sativa – hemp

FERTILITY GIFTS

Brides were often given hazelnuts, said to be a symbol of fertility. This custom was encouraged by the saying: 'Plenty of nuts, plenty of cradles.'

LURING BACK A LOVER

Gypsies traditionally claimed that an acorn, when used as a charm, would bring back an absent lover. To achieve this, the girl needed to gather a sprig of oak with an acorn attached, together with a piece of ash that still had its 'keys' (clustered seed heads). These were put under the girl's pillow for three consecutive nights, while she repeated the following chant several times:

Acorn cup and ashen key,
Bid my true love come to me.
Between moonlight and firelight,
Bring him over the hills tonight:
Over the meadows, over the moor,
Over the rivers, over the sea,
Over the threshold and in at the door.
Acorn cup and ashen key,
Bring my true love back to me.

FLORAL APHRODISIACS

Fewer flowers than vegetables were said to have aphrodisiac qualities, although it was claimed that almost any flower inclined the mind to love.

❧ Orange blossom (*Citrus sinensis*), popular in bridal bouquets and a symbol of pre-marriage chastity, could be infused to create a tonic for nervous brides.

Citrus sinensis

❧ Dog violets or heath violets (*Viola canina*) have long, straggly roots claimed to enhance amorous overtures, while the sweet violet (*Viola odorata*) was used to produce Crème de Violette, a sweet syrup often part of love potions.

Viola odorata

Asphodel

❧ The bulbs of the gladiolus and asphodel were thought to be aphrodisiacs, while a plateful of tulip bulbs was said to 'aid a young man'.

Datura spp.

❀ Thorn apples (*Datura* spp.) have long been medicinal plants with claimed aphrodisiac powers – seeds, when crushed, were applied externally to the sexual organs. In India, *Datura* was widely acclaimed as an aphrodisiac.

❀ Winter cherry (*Withania somnifera*), also known as Indian ginseng, was another plant used in India as an aphrodisiac. Ayurvedic physicians believed that roots of the plant improved a man's sperm count, which led to the claim that powdered root, when taken with milk or clarified butter, acted as an aphrodisiac.

Nicholas Culpeper

PERIWINKLE APHRODISIAC

Nicholas Culpeper (1616–54), English botanist, herbalist and physician, claimed that if leaves and stems of the lesser periwinkle (*Vinca minor*) were 'eaten by a man and wife together, it will cause love between them'.

Vinca minor

A less exciting use of this plant was to tie stems and leaves around the legs to prevent cramp.

WEDDING BOUQUETS

To many brides, bouquets are an essential part of a wedding, making an important status statement. Fashion, however, has influenced the choice of flowers.

Myrtus communis

🌿 Myrtle (*Myrtus communis*) has long been part of bridal bouquets, especially in Mediterranean countries, and it is claimed to have been part of flower arrangements in early Jewish weddings. Greek girls had bridal bouquets of roses combined with myrtle underneath their purple veils.

🌿 Rosemary was once an essential part of bouquets. From the time of Charlemagne (*c.*742–800), brides throughout the Frankish Empire, which covered much of Western and Central Europe, had rosemary in their bouquets.

Rosemary

🌿 Orange blossom bouquets were originated by brides in the East. Later, the idea was taken up European brides.

🌿 White lilac (*Syringa vulgaris*) was popular in bridal bouquets up to the middle of the last century.

Syringa vulgaris

FLORAL BUTTONHOLES

The wearing of a flower in the buttonhole of a lapel in a coat or jacket was mainly a Victorian fashion (although it remains a popular wedding custom). Up until the First World War (1914–18), fashionable men in London often wore a buttonhole; perhaps the most famous of these were the chrysanthemum of the Irish wit, dramatist and poet Oscar Wilde, and the orchid worn by the Liberal politician Joseph Chamberlain.

Prince Albert and family

The origin of the floral buttonhole is not clear. One tenuous suggestion is that Prince Albert took a flower from a bouquet of his wife, Queen Victoria, cut a slit in his tunic and inserted the flower's stem into it.

Oscar Wilde

FERTILITY RITES

It was thought that a stone from a capon's gizzard could make a man into an attractive and virile lover. In some areas, a childless couple would be advised to sleep with the dried testicle of a castrated stallion under their pillows.

WORK AND FAMILY

Human fertility was a major preoccupation in rural communities several hundred years ago. Most people worked on the land, life was physically hard and life expectancy was low. There was therefore an imperative for people to marry early and produce another generation to replenish the labour force.

The birth of babies and their survival were major concerns for country folk, resulting in many wayside and garden plants being bestowed with powers of protection from disease as well as guarding against the Devil, witches and, later, vampires. It was also thought important to use plants – from annual types to trees – to protect farm animals from witches and their spells.

SAVING WOMEN!

The thorny shrub or small tree oleaster (*Elaeagnus angustifolia*), also known as Jerusalem willow or wild olive, which is native to southern Europe and Western Asia, has a form, var. *orientalis*, with especially richly fragrant flowers. In Persia (now Iran), where it was known as *zungeed* or *zinzeyd*, it was claimed to sexually intoxicate women and their emotions. This resulted in men locking up their women when the shrub was flowering.

Elaeagnus angustifolia

PROTECTING INFANTS

At one time, there were many rituals to protect infants from witchcraft and spells cast by the Devil. In some regions, the baby was first bathed before an ash fire, then its head was washed in rum. Giving the baby a drink of cinder tea would also drive the Devil away. This was water into which a hot cinder had been dropped; also, a drink containing sap from an ash tree offered protection.

Scabiosa atropurpurea

MOURNFUL TIMES

The mournful widow (*Scabiosa atropurpurea*), also known as pincushion flower, blackamoor's beauty and sweet scabious, was once worn by widows mourning husbands. Indeed, in the language of flowers it signifies 'I who have lost all'.

APOTHECARY'S ROSE

During the thirteenth century, the town of Provins, south-east of Paris, became famous for an industry that lasted at least 600 years. A red, semi-double rose, *Rosa gallica* var. *officinalis*, became well known for its petals, which had the ability to preserve their scent when dried. It was said that when Marie Antoinette visited Provins in 1770, a bed of rose petals was prepared for her.

This rose was probably one of the first European roses to be introduced to North America and became known for its beauty, scent and medicinal qualities.

HAIR DYE

Women have always loved changing or intensifying the colour of their hair, and throughout the centuries a wide range of plants have been used for this purpose. These include the common barberry (*Berberis vulgaris*), also known as jaundice berry, piprage or pipperidge bush, a hardy deciduous shrub. The roots, or a lye made from the ashes of the whole plant, create a yellow dye. Similarly, a lye of mistletoe results in a yellow shade. The same colour is also gained from the marigold (*Calendula officinalis*).

A decoction of the bark and leaves of box (*Buxus sempervirens*) produces an auburn shade, while henna (*Lawsonia inerma*), when combined with other plant substances, results

in range of colours. This warmth-loving shrub has also been used to dye the palms of hands and soles of feet to cool them and make them more beautiful.

Calendula officinalis

SCENTING LINEN CUPBOARDS

With a name like winter sweet (*Chimonanthus praecox*, earlier known as *C. fragrans*), this deciduous shrub, native to China, has been esteemed for its fragrance. Chinese ladies used the fragrant flowers to decorate their hair, while aromatic twigs were placed in linen cupboards and closets to sweetly perfume the contents.

Bellis perennis

BATTLEFIELD VALUE

The abundant and perennial common daisy (*Bellis perennis*), was said to be a 'measure of love' because lovers pulled off petals to the count of 'He loves me, he loves me not'. A more practical usage, however, was for staunching wounds on the battlefield. The word 'bellis' may

come from a Latin word meaning 'war'; 'perennis' means 'perennial'.

Additionally, the daisy was featured in fairy stories and credited with the power of arresting growth in children to keep them from becoming old.

Ruta graveolens

VINEGAR OF THE FOUR THIEVES

The leaves of rue (*Ruta graveolens*) harbour a powerful irritant which often causes blisters on skin. Rue was credited with the ability to act as an antidote to pestilence. Indeed, it was part of the 'Vinegar of the Four Thieves', a concoction that originated several centuries ago and was said to be so powerful that it enabled thieves in Marseilles to enter and rob homes stricken with the plague, without catching it.

WART LORE

Warts were a consuming interest for people in earlier centuries, with many country cures being attempted. These included cutting notches in an elder stick to correspond with the number of warts on your body, and then burying it. As the stick decayed, so too, it was claimed, did the warts.

In other areas, the afflicted person would approach an ash tree, prick each wart with a new pin and then knock it into the tree's bark, chanting the following rhyme:

Elder

Ashen tree, ashen tree,
Pray buy these warts from me.

Buying warts for a halfpenny from other people was a profitable business for some people and, surprisingly, it often worked.

Ash

Laurus nobilis

CELEBRATORY GARLANDS

The sweet bay or bay laurel (*Laurus nobilis*) was well known to the Romans, who used it in garlands to celebrate victors. Poets of the time were also entitled to wear it as a 'kinde of prophesie or soothsaying'. However, should it quickly wither, this was taken to foretell disaster.

It was also said to provide protection against thunder and lightning, being thought that 'Neither witch nor Devil, thunder nor lightning, will hurt a man in a place where a bay grows'.

FOR GOOD LUCK

Acorns, the small, nut-like fruits produced each year by oak trees, were symbols of immortality and good luck. Carrying an acorn in your pocket was supposed to ensure long life and to guard against disease, especially cholera.

WARDING OFF EVIL SPIRITS

During the Middle Ages, St John's wort (*Hypericum perforatum*), sometimes known as the common St John's wort, was hung over doors on the eve of St John's Day (Midsummer's Eve) to ward off disasters caused by evil spirits.

Additionally, it was credited with other magical properties and could serve as an amulet under a hat or placed under a pillow at night, or used for strewing.

TRAVELLING SAFE

In the *Herbarium* of Apuleius Platonicus, translated into Anglo-Saxon about AD 1000, the merits of using wormwood (*Artemisia absinthium*) were extolled. It recommended holding several sprigs in one hand to reduce the toil of travel.

Artemisia absinthium

In Italy, the supposed benefits of this plant lingered until about 1925: a lorry was seen being driven with a bunch of wormwood tied to its windscreen.

Travellers, Clare Leighton
(1898–1989)

GOOD LUCK, BAD LUCK PLANT!

Mistletoe, with its glistening, white winter berries, was thought to bring good and bad luck. Although sought by lovers wishing to steal a kiss at Christmas, it was considered bad luck to take it into a sacred building.

But lovers had to take care: pieces of mistletoe under which sweethearts had kissed needed to be burned on Twelfth Night (5th January). If not, all those who had kissed under it would be quarrelling before the end of the year!

MAKING INK

In earlier centuries, it was essential to have a home-made ink and several plants were used. Scottish Highlanders used the roots of the yellow flag iris (*Iris pseudacorus*) to make ink. A better-known example is the ink derived from galls on oak trees during the Middle Ages. Indeed, even until quite recent times such ink, variously known as iron gall ink and oak gall ink, has been used for important documents for the United States Treasury and the Bank of England.

The permanence and water-resistance of this ink made it the standard writing material in Europe for over 1,400 years.

Oak gall

ENSURING A WIN

The use of garlic and onions to keep vampires and witches at bay was once widely thought to be prudent, but they were also fastened to the bit of a racehorse in the belief that this would ensure that no horse would pass it.

RUFFING IT

In Elizabethan times, starch made from the bulbs of bluebells (*Hyacinthoides non-scripta*) was used to stiffen ruffs. A glue derived from the bulbs was ideal for securing feathers to arrow shafts.

Hyacinthoides non-scripta

SALAP

During the eighteenth century, the tubers of the early purple orchid (*Orchis mascula*) were dried and powdered and used to make a thin, hot gruel sold under the name of 'salap' or 'saloop' at street stalls and in coffee shops in London. It was believed to be highly nutritious and wholesome, and became exceptionally popular. This, perhaps, was partly due to the tubers' resemblance to testicles, and it was claimed to be an aphrodisiac!

Orchis mascula

SLEEPY PILLOWS

Pillows made of muslin and filled with hop leaves were once recommended as a way to induce sleep, calm nerves and prevent nightmares. Mignonette (*Reseda odorata*) was also used to help facilitate sleep.

Acorus calamus

STREWING HERBS

During the Middle Ages – and up to about the eighteenth century – the use of plants to create a fragrant atmosphere in houses and churches was essential. Bathing was infrequent and people were smelly. The strewing of scented rushes and herbs was necessary not only for their fragrance but also because some of them repelled fleas. Wormwood and pennyroyal (*Mentha pulegium*), for example, were especially effective at combating fleas.

However, it is the sweet flag (*Acorus calamus*), also known as sweet-scented rush, with its fragrant, cinnamon-scented leaves, that remains the best-known strewing plant. One of the charges levied against Cardinal Wolsey by Henry V111, which led to his prosecution in 1529, was his extravagance in strewing floors with this plant.

WOOL AND CLOTH DYES

In the Middle Ages, the dyeing of wool and cloth was a specialized craft which reflected the large and flourishing sheep industry of that time. Many different plants were used as dyes, including heather (*Calluna vulgaris*), which produced a yellow shade, privet for a green colour, and dyer's rocket (*Reseda luteola*) for bright yellow. Dyer's rocket could be mixed with indigo to produce a popular green.

Reseda luteola

Yellow was a popular colour and the roots of meadow rue (*Thalictrum flavum*) were also used; similarly, southernwood (*Artemisia abrotanum*) yielded a yellow dye for wool.

TANNING

During the Middle Ages, most towns had a tanning yard, with many people involved in the craft of processing hides. And because of its smelly nature, this yard was usually situated on the outskirts of a town.

The range of plants used to colour and alter the surface of animal skins over the centuries is wide and included:

❧ Common barberry (*Berberis vulgaris*): Both stems and roots produce a yellow dye. It was widely used in Poland and Morocco to create a beautiful yellow tan.

Berberis vulgaris

❧ Common broom, European broom or Scotch broom (*Cytisus scoparius*): Widely used to tan leather.

❧ Myrtle (*Myrica* spp.): The finest Turkish leather was tanned with the roots of this shrub. Additionally, it imparted a delicate fragrance to the skins.

❧ Tanner's sumac, elm-leafed sumac or Sicilian sumac (*Rhus coriaria*): Leaves and bark were used in the tanning of Turkish and Moroccan leathers.

❧ Ling or Scots heather (*Calluna vulgaris*): In the eighteenth century it was widely used to tan leather, as well as to produce orange and yellow dyes.

❧ Birch (*Betula* spp.): The bark is astringent and was widely used in tanning, where it imparted a distinctive fragrance to Russian leather.

❧ Cañaigres, ganagra, wild rhubarb or tanner's dock (*Rumex hymenosepalus*): Native to western North America, it contains large amounts of tannin and was used by Native Americans for tanning and softening buckskin.

❧ Wattle bark (*Acacia* spp.): The bark of several species – including the black wattle, silver wattle and blackwood – is rich in tannin. The bark was widely used in the Antipodes, as well as being sold to tanneries in Europe. In London, in the 1800s, it fetched £9–11 a ton.

❧ Tanekaha (*Phyllocladus trichomanoides*): This New Zealand native conifer was used to tan and dye kid gloves, producing a fashionable orange-yellow shade.

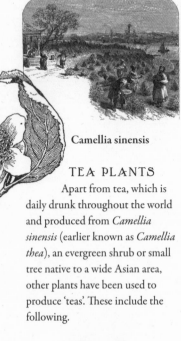

Camellia sinensis

TEA PLANTS

Apart from tea, which is daily drunk throughout the world and produced from *Camellia sinensis* (earlier known as *Camellia thea*), an evergreen shrub or small tree native to a wide Asian area, other plants have been used to produce 'teas'. These include the following.

Ceanothus americanus

❧ New Jersey tea, wild snowball or mountain sweet (*Ceanothus americanus*), a deciduous shrub native to eastern and central states of North America, has leaves which when dried produce a delicious tea. It was used to create a tea during the American Revolutionary War (1775–83), also known as the American War of Independence. Additionally, it was used by Native Americans and a corruption of its native name is 'pong-pong tea'.

❧ Celestial tea or tea of heaven is made from the hydrangea (*Hydrangea serrata* var. *thunbergii*). The fermented leaves are very sweet and are used to make a tea for use in Buddhist ceremonies. Images of the Buddha were bathed in it on his birthday, thereby gaining it the name 'celestial tea'.

❧ Poppy tea is made from the opium poppy (*Papaver somniferum*), a plant native to Western Asia and South East Asia. Opium is a notorious addictive drug but earlier it was used as an alternative 'tea'.

Papaver somniferum

In 1823 it was said that a solution of opium in spirits of wine was used as a tea substitute in many English manufacturing

**The Mad Hatter's tea party,
Alice's Adventures in Wonderland,
Lewis Carroll, 1865**

towns and cities during the
Industrial Revolution (from the
mid-eighteenth to mid-nineteenth
centuries).

❧ Paraguay tea, also known as maté
and yerba maté, is created from *Ilex
paraguariensis*, an evergreen tree
native to South America. When
preparing the leaves for use in a tea,
they are first partly dried in the sun,
making sure that they do not burn,
then steeped, together with twigs, in
hot water (not boiling). Sometimes,
a group of people may drink the
resulting infusion through straws.

EARLY OLYMPIC STIMULANT

The opium poppy (*Papaver
somniferum*) is well known
for its narcotic properties, but
athletes in training for the
Olympic Games in Ancient
Greece are known to have eaten
poppy seeds mixed with wine
and honey to enhance their
performance on the track.

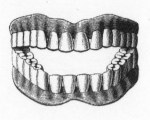

STRENGTHENING GUMS

Columbine or granny's bonnets (*Aquilegia vulgaris*), native to Europe, North Africa, China and temperate Asia, as well as naturalized in North America, was regarded as a remedy for quinsy in the fourteenth century. Later, a tincture was used to strengthen gums, although excessive amounts could be a danger to health!

Aquilegia vulgaris

STRENGTHENING TEETH

English lavender (*Lavandula angustifolia*) is famed for its scented qualities in gardens, homes, boudoirs and posies, but was once used as a mouthwash for people with loose teeth and bad breath.

Lavandula angustifolia

WHITENING TEETH

Flashing teeth and generous smiles have always been in demand, especially for those in search of a partner. Several plants have aided this desire, perhaps none more so than spearmint (*Mentha spicata*), used in the fourteenth century to whiten teeth. However, the Romans used a combination of spearmint and pennyroyal (*Mentha pulegium*) to revive those who had suffered a fainting fit.

Sweet flag (*Acorus calamus*) has been used as an ingredient in toothpastes, as has sage (*Salvia officinalis*). Sage leaves and sea salt were rubbed together and then baked. When crushed and powdered, this was claimed to be able to take away yellow film and stains on teeth. However, Bedouin Arabs are said to have used just sage leaves.

CURING TOOTHACHE

Countryside cures for easing toothache abounded during earlier centuries, when almost every village and town had its own particular cure.

Daphne mezereum

❧ The mezereon (*Daphne mezereum*), European and temperate Asian species, has roots which when dried had a reputation for curing toothache. Indeed, in the 1700s and early 1800s, gardeners near London cultivated this shrub, producing large roots that could be sold to druggists.

❧ The Spanish chamomile or pellitory of Spain (*Anacyclus pyrethrum*) has roots that when chewed ease toothache, deadening the nerves.

❧ The wild marjoram (*Origanum vulgare*) yields an essential oil once used in the alleviation of toothache.

EARACHE AND TOOTHACHE

Liquorice (*Glycyrrhiza glabra*) has been employed medicinally for more than 3,000 years and Native Americans used the roots to cure toothache. They also steeped the leaves in boiling water, allowed the liquid to cool completely and applied it as drops to ease earache.

TOOTHPICKS

For centuries, people without the benefit of a toothbrush had to pick food from their teeth. The common spindle tree (*Euonymus europaeus*), native to Europe and Western Asia and also known as pricklewood, has close-grained wood that can be cut and tailored into toothpicks. It was also used to make skewers, with the wood cut when the tree was in flower and when the strength of the wood was claimed to be at its greatest.

Other uses for the wood were as spindles, bows for musical instruments and toothing for machines. It was still in use for piano and organ keys in the nineteenth century.

THATCHING

In previous centuries, thatching was a major and widespread activity, with local materials invariably taking precedence over those difficult to transport over long distances. Reeds and straws were popular, while unusual materials such as common broom or Scotch broom (*Cytisus scoparius*), heather and yellow flag (*Iris pseudacorus*) were also used.

Ulex europaeus

WHISKERY HORSES

Faggots of gorse, when crushed in mills to break up their spines, were used as fodder for cattle and horses. This led to an amusing suggestion that it encouraged horses to develop long whiskers on their lips, producing an aged appearance.

BAKERS' OVENS

The abundance of gorse (*Ulex europaeus*) on heaths led to it being used as a fuel for bakers' ovens at one time, where it burned quickly and ferociously, giving off a great deal of heat.

GOLD MINING

The Roman Pliny the Elder (AD 23–79) wrote that when collecting gold, trenches were dug and filled with layers of gorse (*Ulex europaeus*). Water containing gold was channelled along the trench, and the gold attached itself to the gorse.

TOBACCO PIPES

Whether as smoking vessels or as a way for young men to impress potential girlfriends, wooden pipes have been popular for several centuries.

Traditional briar pipes were made from the roots of the tree heath (*Erica arborea*), a native of south-west Europe, Mediterranean regions and North Africa. In the late 1800s and early 1900s, large, gnarled roots were dug out of boggy ground and kept in humid sheds to prevent them becoming dry and cracking. When required, they were cut into large pieces and boiled for eight to ten hours to prevent the pipes subsequently made from them from starting to crack. Later, the wood was slowly dried until ready to be cut and carved into pipes.

Briar wood, Corsica, 1923

COUNTRYSIDE SMOKES

Traveller's joy (*Clematis vitalba*) become known as smoking cane, Gypsies' bacca and shepherd's delight on account of its short stems being cut by country people, ignited at one end and smoked.

Clematis vitalba

Thalictrum flavum

CURING ULCERS

The common meadow rue (*Thalictrum flavum*), native to Europe and temperate Asia, was recommended by Pliny the Elder (AD 23–79) as a way to heal ulcers: leaves were coated with honey and then applied to the ulcer.

CONTROLLING LICE

The common, field or forking larkspur (*Delphinium consolida*) is an annual native in Europe and Western Asia. It was introduced into North America and because the whole plant, including the flowers, contains an acid substance, it was used during the American Civil War (1861–65) as a remedy to control body lice.

Delphinium consolida

CURING VENEREAL DISEASES

The North American blue cardinal flower or great lobelia (*Lobelia siphilitica*), with large, intensely blue flowers, was used by Native Americans as a remedy for all types of venereal disease.

DOCTRINE OF SIGNATURES

During the sixteenth century, the Doctrine of Signatures was popularized by the Swiss-German physician and alchemist Paracelsus (1493–1541). This was often known as 'like-for-like' or 'mimetic' magic.

The philosophy he advocated claimed that the medicinal value of any natural substance is indicated by its character, for example, a plant's shape or colour. This was said to be the signature or stamp of a guardian angel.

The logic of this philosophy suggested that the spotted leaves of lungwort (*Pulmonaria officinalis*) were a cure for pulmonary complaints; that plants with yellow flowers or roots with yellow sap controlled jaundice; and that red-coloured roots were ideal for blood disorders.

Lobelia siphilitica

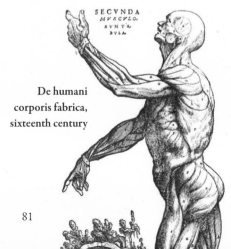

De humani corporis fabrica, sixteenth century

KEEPING WITCHES AT BAY

Many plants are associated with witches, especially with keeping them away! The following plants would keep people safe.

❧ If a juniper bush was planted by the door of a house, no witch was able to enter as first she was obliged to stop and count all the tiny leaves.

❧ Elder leaves were used to make green patterns on floors to deter witches. Additionally, a branch of elder was often buried with a corpse.

❧ Garlic was employed to repel witches, as well as to hold diseases at bay, which were often considered to be part of a witch's arsenal.

❧ Antirrhinums, often known as snapdragons, calves' snouts and lion's mouths, were claimed to preserve a man from being bewitched when hung in bunches indoors, but whether bewitched by women or witches is not quite clear!

❧ Paeony seeds were declared to be a charm against witchcraft; they were also used to prevent nightmares.

❧ Mountain ash was hung above doors of cow houses to repel 'evil eyes'. A sprig placed in a pocket kept the wearer free from spells.

SAVING HORSES FROM WITCHCRAFT

For many centuries, the saving of people and animals from witchcraft was almost an industry. One method for safeguarding horses in country areas was to make a collar of holly (*Ilex aquifolium*) and bittersweet (*Solanum dulcamara*), a widespread clambering and sprawling native plant with poisonous, egg-shaped, green then yellow and later red, berries.

Solanum dulcamara

Ilex aquifolium

LIGHTNING PROTECTION

The widespread mugwort (*Artemisia vulgaris*), native to Europe, Asia and North Africa, has several witchcraft and magic associations. If hung over a door on Midsummer's Day (about 21st June), it was said to ward off lightning, while a spray of its foliage kept indoors would scare away the Devil.

It was also claimed that if a walker put mugwort in his shoes in the morning, he would be able to walk for 40 miles before noon without becoming weary!

Artemisia vulgaris

SNAKES BEWARE

The North American Virginian snakeroot (*Aristolochia serpentaria*) was supposed to cure the bite of a rattlesnake, as well as being 'so offensive to these reptiles, that they not only avoid the places where it grows, but even flee from a traveller who carries a piece of the plant in his hand'.

Egyptian snake charmers were said to use a species of this plant to stupefy snakes before handling them.

SOAPY TALE

Soapwort, also known as bouncing bet, fuller's herb, latherwort and crow-soap (*Saponaria officinalis*) is a scented native of Europe, but was introduced into North America, where it now colonizes many sidewalks and neglected areas. As well as once being used to scour pots and pewter vessels, leaves were used to make a poultice for abrasions and cuts. Soapwort was also considered to be a remedy for jaundice and disorders of the liver.

BEGGAR'S DELIGHT

One way for beggars to extract sympathy from passers-by and to relieve them of money was to raise sores and ulcers on exposed skin. The acrid sap from traveller's joy (*Clematis vitalba*), also known as old man's beard, was painted on arms and hands for this purpose.

Daphne mezereum

Similarly, the bark – and especially the outer covering of roots – of *Daphne mezereum*, widely known as the February daphne and mezereon, was also used externally to raise blisters.

Saponaria officinalis

MUSICAL BAMBOOS

Bamboos have a long history of being used to make musical instruments and are frequently employed in recorders (pipe-like instruments). In the Malacca Islands, natives pierced the stems of growing bamboos in such a way as to produce attractive, flute-like notes. Some stems were pierced several times and in a breeze would produce up to twenty different notes. The natives named these living orchestras as *bulu perindu* (plaintive bamboos.)

Straits of Malacca

BAMBOO BICYCLES

Bamboo canes are widely used in furniture construction, while in the 1890s bicycles and tricycles were constructed from them and praised for their rigidity, strength and comfort.

Helianthus annuus

LIFEBELT PADDING

The sunflower (*Helianthus annuus*), an annual native of Central America and well known for its oil-yielding seeds, has pith in its stems, once used to fill lifebelts, being the lightest substance then known.

BLAZING A TRAIL

An interesting North American story about creating a trail for others to follow is associated with the Mormons, when they left Missouri to search for a place where they could worship God in their own way.

As they travelled, it is said that they scattered seeds of the common sunflower or mirasol (*Helianthus annuus*) – probably originally a Mexican plant but now widely seen growing wild throughout North America – so that people travelling during the following year could easily follow them. These 'sunflower trails' produced brightly coloured yellow and orange flowers that could be discerned even in early twilight.

TORCHES

The Romans dipped the stems of the yellow mullein (*Verbascum thapsus*), also known as Aaron's rod, hag taper and torches, in tallow and burned them as torches. The name 'hag taper' derives from this plant's use in sorcery.

Verbascum thapsus

CHAPTER EIGHT

Weather Folklore

Predicting the nature of forthcoming weather through rhymes and stories was a central part of rural life when many people could not read. Such weather interpretations were often passed down through generations and although they were not steeped in scientific fact, they were often correct. This should not be surprising as people who daily 'work the land' are usually acutely aware of the best times to sow or plant crops, as well as when to harvest them.

**Storm, Paul Landacre
(1893–1963)**

ONION PREDICTORS

This rhyme relied on the appearance of onions after harvesting, usually some time from midsummer to early autumn.

> *Onion skin very thin,*
> *Mild winter coming in,*
> *Onion skin thick and tough,*
> *Coming winter cold and rough.*

GROUNDHOG DAY

This North American prophesy relied on the groundhog, a rodent variously known as woodchuck, whistle-pig and land beaver, being able to see its own shadow on 2nd February. According to folklore, if the weather was cloudy on this day and when the groundhog emerged from its burrow, spring would

come early. But if it was sunny, the animal would see its own shadow and retreat back into its burrow, indicating that winter weather would continue for several more weeks.

PLOUGHING

Some rhymes advise on the best time to plough and often were related to specific geographic areas. For example, in the Bristol area of Britain, the state of the sea in the Bristol Channel was taken as an indication of when to plough:

> *If it raineth when it doth flow,*
> *Then yoke your ox and go to plough,*
> *But if it raineth when it doth ebb,*
> *Unyoke your ox and go to bed.*

A variation of this rhyme in North America was:

> *Raining on the flood,*
> *Nothing but a scud [a shower],*
> *Raining on the ebb,*
> *Might as well go to bed.*

BEE LORE

Bees were an integral part of country life. The honey they produced was especially valued as a sweetener and a way to preserve food. Their flight patterns and habits were particularly watched and noted as predictors of changing weather. For example:

> *If bees stay at home,*
> *Rain will soon come,*
> *If they fly away,*
> *Fine will be the day.*

PLANT WEATHER LORE

Trees and shrubs were frequently featured in old weather sayings and these include:

If the oak's before the ash,
You will only get a splash,
But if the ash precedes the oak,
You will get a soak.

Holly berries shining red,
Mean a long winter, 'tis said.

Beware the oak, it draws the stroke;
Avoid the ash, it courts the flash;
Creep under a thorn,
it can save you from harm.

SEASONAL INDICATORS

The seasonal festivals were closely linked to weather guidance. The following rhymes relate to Candlemas (2nd February): the weather on this day was believed to point to what lay ahead. Incidentally, in earlier years, many people understood the Christmas season to last for 40 days, until 2nd February.

If Candlemas Day be fair and bright,
Winter will have another flight,
If Candlemas Day be clouds and rain,
Winter be gone and will not come again.

On Candlemas Day if the thorns
hang adrop,
You can be sure of a good pea crop.

Some rhymes relating to Candlemas warn that winter weather may not have passed and bad weather could be expected:

A farmer should, on Candlemas Day,
Have half his corn and half his hay.

*When Candlemas day is cloudy
and black,
It always hugs winter away on
its back.*

The rhymes appear in various countries. An English one cites Yorkshire wisdom:

*In Yorkshire ancient people say,
If February's second day
Be fair and clear,
It doth portend a scanty year
For hay and grass, but if it rains
They never then perplex their brains.*

**Woodcut, Clare Leighton
(1898–1989)**

Good Friday and Easter Day also had their share of weather predictions, including:

*Rain on Good Friday
or Easter Day,
A good crop of grass
but a bad one of hay.*

LUNAR FORECASTS

The moon held magical implications for country folk, who keenly watched its changes. This gave rise to several cultivation rhymes, including:

*If the moon shows a silver shield,
Be not afraid to reap your field,
But if she rises haloed round,
Soon we'll tread on deluged ground.*

*The moon and the weather
may change together,
But a change of the moon
will not change the weather.*

*A ring around the moon or sun
Means rain or snow coming soon.*

Seagull, seagull, get this on t' sand,
It'll never be fine
while thou'rt on t' land.

When seagulls fly to land,
A storm is at hand.

BOVINE WEATHER FORECASTERS

Cows prefer not to have the wind blowing in their faces, thus originating the following weather rhyme:

A cow with its tail to the west,
makes the weather the best,
A cow with its tail to the east,
makes the weather the least.

BIRDS

The activities of birds were seen to be connected to the weather, for example:

On the first of March,
The crows begin to search;
By the first of April,
They are sitting still;
By the first of May,
They've all flown away,
Coming greedy back again,
With October's wind and rain.

MIST AND FOG

These seasonal occurrences generated several apt rhymes.

For every fog in March,
There'll be a frost in May.
A northern harr [mist] brings
Fine weather from afar.

When mist comes from the hill,
Then good weather it doth spill;
When the mist comes from the sea,
Then good weather it will be.

SUNRISE AND SUNSET

Perhaps the best-known rhyme
about sunrise and sunset is the first
one below:

> *A red sky in the morning*
> *Is a shepherd's warning.*
> *A red sky at night*
> *Is a shepherd's delight.*

> *If the sun goes pale to bed,*
> *'Twill rain tomorrow, it is said.*

CLOUDS AND SKY

Several of these weather omens have
proved themselves to be accurate for
many centuries, and include:

> *Mackerel sky,*
> *Not long dry.*

> *When clouds appear*
> *like rocks and towers,*
> *The earth's refreshed*
> *by frequent showers.*

> *If a rainbow comes at night,*
> *The rain will be gone quite.*

> *Rain before seven,*
> *Fine before eleven.*

> *When clouds look like black smoke,*
> *A wise man will put on his cloak.*

> *A rainbow afternoon,*
> *Good weather coming soon.*

> *If clouds move against the wind,*
> *Rain will follow.*

DITCHES AND PONDS

The state of ditches and ponds was believed to be linked to future weather:

When the ditch and pond
offend the nose,
Then look out for rain
and stormy blows.

Woodcut, Robert Gibbings
(1889–1958)

SMOKE

Even the way that smoke rose from a hearth or bonfire was considered to predict forthcoming weather:

When smoke hovers
close to the ground,
There will be a weather change.

Chimney smoke descends,
Our nice weather ends.

When down the chimney
falls the soot,
Mud will soon be underfoot.

STORMS

Storm lore is varied, but the harbingers of approaching wet weather were considered to be:

❧ Birds chirp louder.

❧ Cats clean themselves and increasingly meow.

❧ Clover folds up its leaves.

❧ Cows and sheep huddle together, seeking comfort.

GRAFTING

Guidance on the best time of the year to graft fruit trees was steeped in ritual and many indications were said to be given by the moon. It was claimed that grafts were more successful if grafting was undertaken when the moon was waxing (moving towards a full moon).

Thomas Tusser (1524–80), English poet and farmer, suggested:

> *From moon being changed,*
> *Till past be the prime,*
> *For grafting and cropping*
> *Is a very good time.*

Many types of grafting were popular: some completely changed the variety, others just altered a few branches. In 'approach' grafting, two branches were united and later separated when the union had been successful.

🌿 Dandelions close their blooms.

🌿 Horses 'twitch and switch', and sometimes bolt.

🌿 Insects fly lower and bite more and frequently.

🌿 Morning glories tuck in their flowers

CHAPTER NINE

Pest and Disease Folklore

In earlier centuries, pests and diseases were often thought to be acts of God and were accepted as a part of life. However, preventive measures and cures did abound in country areas and some are still superb for keeping plants 'clean'. Indeed, many of these measures have a 'green' nature and do not damage the environment.

it is essential to remember that they are mammals and must only be killed in a humane manner. Better still, deter them by planting caper spurge (*Euphorbia lathyrus*) near their runs.

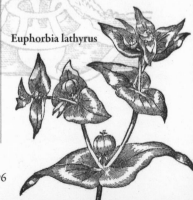

Euphorbia lathyrus

APHIDS

Where infestations of greenfly (aphids) were few in number and especially when on delicate flowers, aphid brushes became popular for removing the aphids.

MOLES

During earlier times, mole traps were often used to brutally despatch these tunnelling garden delinquents, but nowadays, with animal welfare legislation in force,

WIREWORMS

Large, decaying pieces of carrot or potato tubers were shallowly buried along rows of newly sown vegetables to attract wireworms into them. Later, these were removed and burned.

CARROT ROOT FLY

These pests are attracted to carrots by their smell. Earlier preventives included placing strips of rag soaked in paraffin (kerosene) between rows to confuse them. Interplanting rows of carrots and garlic also confused this pest.

OLD BUCKET MOUSETRAP

Where an old, small bucket was available, the handle was removed and a stout spindle placed across the top.

Centred on the spindle was a rotating, tooth-edged wheel that attracted mice as it spun. A mouse investigating it invariably fell into water contained in the bucket and was later killed as humanely as possible.

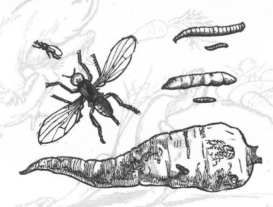

Carrot root fly

EARWIGS

Earwigs love concealing themselves, especially during daytime. A flowerpot filled with straw or dried grass and inverted on a bamboo cane inserted among border plants is still a good way to trap them. Each morning, remove the straw and terminate the earwigs.

LEATHERJACKETS

An earlier – and still effective – way to control leatherjackets in lawns was to thoroughly water the surface and then cover it overnight with sacking. Leatherjackets rise to the surface and in the morning can be either swept off or left to the attention of birds.

Another early trap was a small box with a funnel-shaped piece of glass fitted into the top. Earwigs investigating the box fell in and could be killed the following morning.

BIRDS

Birds cause damage to flowers, young shoots and fruits, and a cherry clacker was part of a gardener's arsenal in scaring them away. Basically, it was formed of a propeller that turned a spindle, causing pieces of wood to snap together and emit a series of sharp clacking noises.

RABBITS

To deter rabbits from chewing bark, sticks were placed around a tree's trunk and bound with tarred cord.

MICE

In spring, mice especially scavenge for food. To prevent them getting at seeds sown in vegetable gardens, short pieces of gorse were put in the sown drills before covering with soil.

COCKROACHES

These pernicious pests caused especial damage to tender plants in heated greenhouses. Jam jars sunk to their rims and quarter-filled with a mixture of beer and sugar lured them to their deaths.

VINE WEEVILS AND EARWIGS

Sacking, placed overnight on the floor or staging of a greenhouse, was used to lure and entrap vine weevils and earwigs. Each morning, the pests were shaken or picked off the sacking and destroyed.

WASP TRAPS

Wasps soon destroy ripening fruits, especially when grown against a warm, sheltered wall. At one time, bottle traps, a quarter-full of a mixture of beer, water and sugar, were suspended from branches. The mouth of the bottle needed a deep shoulder against which wasps would strike when attempting to fly out.

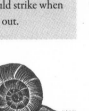

SLUGS AND SNAILS

Slugs and snails have always been major pests and one early deterrent is still good: scatter broken eggshells around plants.

SAFEGUARDING ROSES

Members of the tit family could be
encouraged to eat aphids on roses
by inserting bamboo canes, 1.8 m
(6 ft) long, slantwise among rose
bushes and securing 7.5–10 cm
(3–4 in.) pieces of fat to their ends.
The fat attracted tits, which then
scavenged for greenfly.

PICKLE-JAR
MOUSETRAP

Apart from eating seeds, mice
nibble and bite at almost anything.

One type of early
trap involved
liberally smearing
the inside rim of
a jar with lard or

grease, then burying it up to its rim
in soil. The jar was half-filled with

water. Inquisitive mice then fell into
the water and later were killed as
humanely as possible.

ANTS

Ripening fruits on wall-trained
fruit trees were protected from ants
by inscribing a broad band of chalk
along the bottom of a wall and
around the base of trees.

WOOLLY APHIDS

Also known as American blight,
the woolly aphid creates a mass
of white, wool-like wax on fruit
trees. A lather of soft soap was
used to coat affected areas in
winter. If the problem reoccurred
in spring, paraffin was brushed
into the tree's crevices.

GREENHOUSE APHIDS

A dramatic cure was to heat a large, flat piece of iron until it was red-hot and then to place cayenne pepper on it (with the proviso to close all ventilators and to exit the greenhouse immediately). The fumes were claimed to kill aphids.

DANGEROUS BREW

Quassia chips, derived from the South American, Caribbean and Mexican tree *Quassia amara* and widely known as bitterwood, were used to make a toxic brew to kill aphids and caterpillars. It was said to have the advantage of not killing bees.

Another brew for killing greenfly was a mixture of rhubarb and elder leaves, while a fomentation of elder leaves on their own prevented mildew.

GREENFLY BEWARE

Repeatedly syringing the leaves and stems of plants with tobacco or lime water was claimed to remove greenfly.

EARWIG STICKS

Hollow pieces of elder, the pith having been removed and about 15 cm (5 in. long), were laid horizontally on branches and in different parts of a tree. Earwigs hid in them and, in the morning, could be killed as humanely as possible.

SHOE TRAPS

Old shoes filled with straw were put at the bases of trees as lures for earwigs. Each morning, the straw and earwigs were removed and burned.

SNAIL AND SLUG CONTROL

To prevent slugs and snails from climbing a wall to reach plants, a paste-like mixture of thick oil and soot was painted along the bottom of the wall.

COCKROACHES BEWARE

The moth mullein (*Verbascum blattaria*), a biennial plant native to Europe and Western and Central Asia, as well as naturalized in North America, was used as a cockroach repellent. Indeed, the scientific classification of the cockroach comes from the word 'blattaria'.

Verbascum blattaria

RATS AND MICE

Nearly 2,000 years ago the Roman author, naturalist and philosopher Pliny the Elder claimed that the garden flower *Asphodelus*, known as king's spear and asphodel, would 'chase away rats and mice'.

Asphodelus

Urginea maritima

POTENT RAT POISON

Scilla maritima (now *Urginea maritima* and sometimes referred to as *Drima maritima*) is a bulbous Mediterranean plant known as sea squill, red squill and sea onion; it was claimed to produce one of the deadliest rat poisons.

ROMAN WEEDKILLER

During the last century BC, Marcus Terentius Varro, widely considered at that time to be the most learned of all Romans and who wrote *De Agricultura* (an agricultural treatise), described the use of the residue from olives (after the oil had been extracted) as a weedkiller. This residue has a high salt concentration and would kill plants by preventing them absorbing water.

SCARING BIRDS

Apart from cherry clackers, perhaps the best-known bird-scarer is the scarecrow, which has a human-like form and is usually dressed in cast-off clothing. However, not all birds are frightened off by its appearance: some species frequently use scarecrows as perches.

In Japan, a scarecrow known as Kuebiko was mentioned in a book known as *Kojiki* (dating from the early eighth century and said to be the 'Record of Ancient Matters'). Kuebiko, the god of knowledge and agriculture, is represented as a scarecrow who cannot walk but has complete awareness.

FROGS AND TOADS

In times gone by, frogs and toads were seen as keepers of secrets, participants in transformations, who know the secret of eternal life. In ancient Chinese legends, the toad was thought to be a trickster and magician, a master of escapes and spells. While some 2,000 years ago, the Roman writer Pliny the Elder claimed that a toad would silence a room full of people. Tribes in South and Central America used chemical compounds from toads and frogs as poisons and hallucinogenic drugs during their religious rituals.

But all of these claims are slightly unfair to these amphibians who help to keep gardens free from slugs.

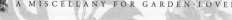
CHAPTER TEN

The World of Garden Gnomes

Garden gnomes are usually loved or loathed, while some people consider them to be features solely of amusement. Nevertheless, they can be seen in many gardens, either singly or in family groups. And that they are here to stay is not in doubt.

Paracelsus

botanist, alchemist and astrologer Paracelsus (1493–1541). He classified them as 'earth elements', describing them as two spans high, reluctant to associate with people and able to move through solid earth as easily as humans pass through air.

PARACELSUS

The 'birth' of the gnome is not clear, although gnome aficionados point out that they appeared early in the sixteenth century in the writings of the Swiss-German physician,

ANCESTRY

The heritage of gnomes is much debated, with speculation that they are descendants of the Graeco-Roman fertility god Priapus, sometimes Priapos, protector of fruit plants, livestock and gardens.

FRENCH DEVELOPMENTS

In about 1616, Jacques Callot (1592–1635) engraved and printed figures of a gobbi (dwarf). These images must have had great appeal: by the late eighteenth century, porcelain gnomes, known as house dwarfs, were being produced.

Jacques Callot

GERMAN INFLUENCE

The date of the manufacture of early garden gnomes (also known as lawn gnomes) is disputed, but the company Baehr and Maresch of Dresden, Germany, had produced ceramic outdoor gnomes by 1841. And from about 1860, gnomes were made in Thuringia, an area christened in the late nineteenth century as the 'green heart of Germany'.

ENGLISH ADVENTURE

Gnomes were introduced into Britain in 1847 by Sir Charles Edmund Isham (1819–1903), a landowner and gardener, with 21 terracotta figures brought back from a trip to Germany. He was a bonsai enthusiast and made an early collection of these dwarfed plants, populating them with his 'little people'.

STORYBOOK GNOMES

These colourful creatures have often been portrayed in fantasy literature, where a wide range of characters have appeared, for instance in the following books:

❧ *The Chronicles of Narnia* by C. S. Lewis (1898–1963). Here gnomes are known as Earthmen, living in the Underland, and are used as slaves by the Lady of the Green Kirtle, also known as Queen of the Underland.

❧ *The Father Christmas Letters* by J. R. R. Tolkien (1892–1973) tells of the adventures and misadventures of Father Christmas and his helpers, including Red Gnomes who travelled from Norway to the North Pole to assist him.

❧ The Harry Potter stories by J. K. Rowling (b. 1965) feature mischievous but harmless gnomes who inhabit the gardens of witches and wizards.

❧ *The Little Grey Men*, written and illustrated under the nom de plume 'BB' (Denys James Watkins-Pitchford, 1905–90), tells of the exploits of four gnomes named after flowers: Baldmoney, Sneezewort, Dodder and Cloudberry.

❧ The Oz series of books, which began with *The Wonderful Wizard of Oz* (1900), were written by an American author of children's books, Lyman Frank Baum (1856–1919). These books were populated with many invented characters – *Kabumpo in Oz* (1922) featured Ruggedo the gnome king (originally spelled 'nome' by Baum), who turns into a giant while tunnelling under the Emerald City.

FAME AND ESTABLISHMENT

Loved, hated or just tolerated, ceramic gnomes have, for many people, become the guardians of gardens. For some devotees, their garden is more of a gnome theme park. Ann Atkin, founder of the world-famous Gnome Reserve in Devon, south-west England, may

GNOMES' EVOLUTION

During the late 1800s, the underground and tunnelling nature of the gnome began to change in children's stories and they became more associated with the 'little people', including goblins, elves, leprechauns and brownies.

Illustrations of gnomes in storybooks usually depicted them as bearded males, with red hats and often a smoking pipe. In more recent times, female gnomes have been introduced.

have the world's largest known population of these characters, where they inhabit woodland glades and sit by flowery paths. Visitors are often offered the loan of a pointed gnome's cap to wear so that 'the gnomes think you are one of them'.

GNOMES BLACKBALLED

Gnomes pop up in many gardens, tastefully positioned in grottoes or near water features to add character and fun, but you will not see them at the Royal Horticultural Society's Chelsea Flower Show in London, an annual event in the gardening calendar.

Much to the chagrin of gnome enthusiasts, the RHS considers gnomes to detract from flower displays and attractive garden designs, and has banned them.

MISCHIEVOUS GOBLINS

Goblins, often associated with brownies and gnomes, possess magical abilities, although they use them in a mischievous manner. Goblins were said to be 45–60 cm 1½–2 ft) tall, thin, bald and brown, but this varies from one country to another and in literature they are often depicted as clever, arrogant, greedy and churlish.

They are widely featured in storybooks, from Enid Blyton's Noddy stories to Harry Potter tales and J. R. R. Tolkien's *The Hobbit* and *The Lord of the Rings*. So keep a look out for them!

CHAPTER ELEVEN

Down on the Farm

When wild grasses and some animals became domesticated about 10,000 years ago, for most people – but not all – a nomadic life that had existed for 50,000 or more years slowly ended. Hunter-gatherers, who earlier had lived in groups of ten to 50 people, following the seasons and surviving on animals they hunted, as well as foraged leaves, berries, roots, fruits and nuts, began a settled way of life. There followed the development of hamlets, villages and towns, leading to land being fenced, regularly cultivated and plants harvested. This more assured food supply resulted in a higher birth rate and the cycle of 'birth, life and demand for more food' that still prevails today.

EARLY FARMING

The Fertile Crescent (a wide area between the River Euphrates and River Tigris) in Western Asia was one of the regions where the domestication of animals and food crops began. It also occurred in Egypt, China, India and areas in the Americas.

General and localized climate changes after the Younger Dryas – about 13,000 years ago and, in part, during the latter days of the last major ice age – especially favoured the growth of annual plants, including grass food crops such as rye, maize and rice.

Oryza
sativa – rice

Secale cereale – rye

Lens culinaris – lentil

NEOLITHIC FARMING DEVELOPMENTS

Known as the Later Stone Age or New Stone Age, and lasting from 12,700 to 11,400 years ago, it was not until after this period that the so-called founding crops of agriculture appeared. The first were Emmer and Einkorn types of wheat, then hulled barley, peas, lentils, chickpeas and flax; they were grown on sites bordering the eastern shores of the Mediterranean and the Aegean, especially in areas now known as Syria, Lebanon and Palestine.

BRONZE AGE

By the Bronze Age (about 7,500 to 3,200 years ago), foraged food was becoming an increasingly smaller part of human diets in many areas of the world. The Sumerians are credited as being the 'inventors of agriculture', with farmers producing sufficient food to sustain people not involved in agriculture. This, it is claimed, led to expanding empires, the origination of armies and conflict between regions.

ROMAN FARMING

Roman agriculture was a development of Sumerian agriculture. With an abundance of slaves, the Roman Empire developed the manorial way of farming, essentially based on serfdom, which flourished well into the Middle Ages.

ROMAN AGRICULTURAL SYSTEMS

The Romans had four systems of farm management, depending on the size and fertility of the area farmed. In the first, work was undertaken by the owner and his family. The next involved slaves working under the supervision of a slave manager. The third was tenant farming (a form quite similar to 'sharecropping', a method of farming known in North America), in which the owner and a tenant divide a farm's produce. And the fourth system was where a farm was leased to a tenant.

FARMING IN INDIA

By about 10,000 years ago, India was growing wheat, barley and jujube (an edible, plum-like fruit); the domestication of sheep and goats occurred soon after. The Indians created systems of planting crops in rows, threshing and storing grain in granaries. The irrigation of crops was another major development.

Ziziphus zizyphus – jujube

SOUTH AMERICA AND THE POTATO

In the Andean region of South America, potatoes were first cultivated about 7,000 years ago, with tubers sometimes left outside on rocks for frost to break down their structure. The sun dried them, enabling the floury material

to be stored. Native people also domesticated alpacas, llamas and guinea pigs.

ISLAMIC WORLD

During the eighth century, agricultural practice in the Islamic world underwent a transformation. This was partly influenced by Islamic travellers both gathering and disseminating information along Muslim trade routes, which covered large areas of the Old World. Crops involved in this age of agricultural enlightenment included rice, cotton and sugar cane, also vegetables and fruit trees.

Additionally, agricultural techniques including crop rotation and irrigation were made widely known; some of these were extensions of information known to the Romans.

German illustration of country life, 1470

BRITAIN

The idea of purposely growing food plants spread west across Europe, reaching the coasts of France and Belgium some 6,000 years ago. New food-producing techniques infiltrated into Britain, replacing the hunter-gatherer way of life.

Probably, the first sign of farming in Britain involved Emmer and Einkorn wheats, also barley. Initially, the same crops were continuously grown on the same land for several years, resulting in decreased yields. As a result, many farmers moved to fresh land every few years, but this was seen to be wasteful and, eventually, better soil husbandry techniques were introduced, such as crop rotation and leaving land fallow for a year or so for its fertility to recover.

ROMANS IN BRITAIN

The Roman conquest of the British Isles, which began in AD

43, introduced farming ideas the Romans had inherited from other cultures and countries. But the exchange of agricultural ideas had been happening earlier than this and the Celts in southern and eastern areas of the British Isles were skilled arable farmers by the time the Romans arrived.

BRITISH DEVELOPMENTS

Between the sixteenth and mid-nineteenth centuries, Britain's food output increased dramatically, mainly resulting from mechanization, crop rotation and improved strains of cereals.

EARLY PLOUGHS

The earliest plough was simply an enlarged hoe which stirred the soil as it was dragged along. This type of implement was used in India and

other Eastern countries at least until the middle of the last century.

Ploughs with mouldboards (a curved board or metal plate that turns over earth from a furrow) came into use in Europe before the fourteenth century, but it was not until the eighteenth century that ploughs resembling the modern type were invented.

FOOT PLOUGHS

Foot ploughs, a type of plough used like a spade to cultivate land, were known in many parts of the world in the 1600s. Although cumbersome and heavy to use, it was said in the Scottish Western Isles that a man with a foot plough could do the same amount of work as four men who each had an ordinary spade. Also, a foot plough was claimed to be more practical than a horse-drawn plough when on rocky and stony land.

BREAST PLOUGHS

This was another early way of preparing land for sowing crops and was used both to remove surface grass and to plough small acreages of land. The face of the plough measured 38 x 23 cm (15 x 9 in.), with the right-hand side turned up about 7.5 cm (3 in.) and a cutting edge at its front.

WHEELED PLOUGHS

Ploughs of the early Britons were not as advanced as those in Europe and part of this resulted from the decree that no man should guide a plough until he could make one. Also, Saxon ploughs were drawn in a barbarous fashion by attaching them to the tails of draught oxen.

The Normans made a wheeled plough, but the driver also carried an axe to break up large clods.

DUTCH INFLUENCE

The Dutch were among the first to bring the plough to its present state, with a development that was introduced into northern Britain and later known as the 'Rotherham'. It was basically a wood-framed plough but with a plated mouldboard and sole (underneath part).

Wooden-framed ploughs, rather than those with iron handles and beams (main framework), were particularly valued by early ploughmen as they enabled a sensitive 'feel' for the land.

Wooden plough, Spain

PLOUGH MANUFACTURE

In the mid-1700s, several British companies started to build metal ploughs that were pulled by horses. James Small (1730–93) of Berwickshire, Scotland, began to make iron ploughs and in 1784 took his design to the Carron Iron Works to be cast. It was an immediate success, replacing the existing cumbersome wooden types. He greatly influenced the agricultural revolution; a demonstration of his ploughs was even requested by King 'Farmer' George III (1738–1820).

EAST ANGLIAN INFLUENCE

In 1789, Robert Ransome (1753–1830) set up a small foundry in Norwich, soon moving to Ipswich where, by chance, he discovered the technique of making the surface

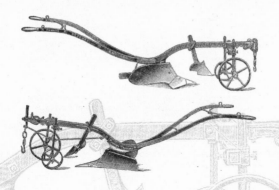

Chilled breast plough, Howard

of cast iron extremely hard. He patented this process as 'Chilled Casting', and it was used to ensure that ploughshares remained sharp.

REFINING WHEELED PLOUGHS

During the 1800s, several British companies refined and improved the wheeled plough, with James Howard and Frederick Howard opening an ironworks in Bedfordshire.

Deep plough, Ransome

DEEP PLOUGHING

Some land needed to be ploughed deeply to break up low 'pans' of hard soil that prevented water draining freely. A design of plough specifically for this purpose had a large furrow wheel and could plough soil to a depth of about 35 cm (14 in.).

SCUFFLER

A scuffler was used for heavy cultivation, including breaking up soil that had remained fallow for several years. Also, it was ideal for ploughing stubble and levelling land left after the removal of large roots. Because the work was heavy, it invariably needed to be drawn by a large and powerful tractor.

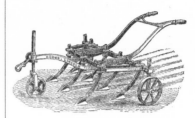

Scuffler, Cooke

General cultivator, Martin

SPRING-TINE CULTIVATOR

This was a much lighter piece of equipment than a scuffler and ideal for shallowly working the soil, disturbing and removing weeds. Additionally, where land had been left with ridges after the removal of an earlier crop, it was well suited to levelling the soil.

HARROW

Harrows were implements for breaking up the soil, creating a tilth and levelling the surface in preparation for sowing seeds or planting crops. They were originally

drawn by draught animals such as horses, mules or oxen; in early times and in some places they were sometimes pulled by labourers!

There were several types of harrow: disc, tine, chain, and chain-disc.

Harrow, Sellar

REAPER AND BINDER

Health and safety on farms has always been an issue but few pieces of equipment were as lethal as a hay mower, with its reciprocating, knife-clad bar that scythed off stems. A reaper and binder, with rotating cutting bars 1.5–1.8 m (5–6 ft) across on horse-drawn models, could also be a lethal piece of equipment.

Harrow, Howard

Reaper and binder, Hornsby

STEAM PLOUGH

Steam plough engine, Fowler

The idea of using steam power to draw a plough across land was a direct result of steam technology that originated and developed during the Industrial Revolution. In the years 1830–50, many patents describing steam cultivation machinery were lodged and in 1854, the Royal Agricultural Society of England offered a prize of £500 for 'the steam cultivator which shall in the most efficient manner turn over the soil and be an economic substitute for the plough or spade'.

A steam engine positioned on the headland of a field could haul a ploughing implement to and fro by means of a wire rope. The advantage of this was that it did not consolidate the ground in the same way that a horse would do as it dragged a plough over the land. However, the depth of ploughing needed careful adjustment to prevent subsoil being turned up and placed above the topsoil.

Portable steam engine, Hornsby

Planet Jr. cultivator

HAND·POWERED TOOLS

Few pieces of horticultural and low-acreage agricultural equipment have been used so widely throughout the world as the Planet Jr. From the 1910s through to the 1950s, this simple, robust and adaptable method of cultivating soil in gardens, backyards and smallholdings had few rivals. However, in the 1960s, industrial farming put many smallholders out of business, although self-sufficiency enthusiasts still use it – and it is relatively inexpensive to buy, long-lasting, adaptable and robust, and does not damage the environment.

Modifications have recently been made to the design and it is enjoying greater use.

SUMMER HARVEST

During the Middle Ages, illustrated calendars were popular, with this harvest scene portrayed in 'Le

Summer, Le Grant Kalendrier de Bergiers, Le Rouge 1496

Divining, De Re Metallica, Agricola, 1556

Grant Kalendrier des Bergiers' by Nicolas le Rouge, Troyes, 1496. It shows men using tooth-edged sickles to cut a cereal crop, which was then tied into bundles by women.

DOWSING FOR WATER

Dowsing (or water divining) is a way to locate underground water, metals, ores, oil and even grave sites. A Y-shaped stick, known as a dowsing rod or divining rod, is held in both hands, with the long end pointing forward to detect underground currents from the soil.

Dowsing for metals is said to have originated in Germany in the fifteenth century. The discovery of metals in this way was described in *De Re Metallica* by Georg Bauer (Georgius Agricola) in 1556.

In 1662, dowsing was claimed to be 'satanic', although in the south of France in the seventeenth century it was used to track criminals and heretics.

Dowsing is best known, however, for the detection of water. In Europe, hazel sticks were mainly used, while in North America it was the witch hazel; peach and willow branches were also employed. Today, some dowsers just use a pair of L-shaped metal rods, one held in each hand.

PIG FARMING

Native to Eurasia and North Africa, pigs were some of the first animals to be domesticated, thought to be 7,000 to 9,000 years ago and possibly in the Middle East, eastern Mediterranean or South East Asia. Most pigs are kept for their delicious meat, although a few are housed as pets with perhaps one of the most famous examples being the Duke of Emsworth's pig, Empress, in the Blandings novels by P. G. Wodehouse.

KEEPING CHICKENS

If you have ever watched chickens in a farmyard or backyard, you will realize how important they feel about themselves – bustling about, scratching the ground or walking with an aristocratic gait. It is estimated that at any one time there are more than 28 billion chickens worldwide and they all originated from wildfowl in South East Asia (and probably Vietnam) about 10,000 years ago.

**The Prodigal Son Among the Pigs,
Albrecht Dürer (1471–1528)**

Woodcut, Julius John Lankes (1884–1960)

They spread to India, then Asia Minor and on to Greece about 7,000 years ago and subsequently to Egypt during the eighteenth dynasty (1550–1292 BC).

A chicken's egg is one of the miracles of nature and although primarily intended for reproduction of the species, eggs have been hijacked by millions of people each day as an invaluable source of protein. Additionally, medical research suggests that eating eggs may prevent age-related macular degeneration of the eyes.

121

CHAPTER TWELVE

Early Lawns

Early references to lawns appeared in Giovanni Boccaccio's
Decameron, mainly completed in 1352, and in a late version of Le
Roman de la Rose, an allegory of courtly love and romance of the
thirteenth century. However, medieval lawns were not the pure
grass swards that are now fashionable, but meadow grass peppered
with wild flowers, some growing quite tall.

LAYING A LAWN

The Italian Pietro de' Crescenzi
(c.1230–1320) gave instructions
for the construction of a turf
lawn in his *Opus Liber Ruralium
Commodorum* (The Advantages of
Rural Living). He recommended
digging out all weeds, scalding the
soil with boiling water to prevent
weed seeds germinating and then
laying turf brought in from the
wild. This was to be beaten and
trodden into place until the grass
almost disappeared, then allowed to
produce new shoots.

Chamaemelum nobile

CHAMOMILE LAWNS

When John Evelyn (1620–1706),
the English garden designer
and diarist, wrote about the
maintenance of lawns, he
was referring to the fragrant,
mat-forming chamomile

Giovanni Boccaccio

(*Chamaemelum nobile*, formerly *Anthemis nobilis*). It has finely dissected, mid-green leaves and can be used to form a decorative, but not hard-wearing, lawn.

FRANCIS DRAKE

Legend suggests that Sir Francis Drake (*c.*1540–96) played bowls on a chamomile lawn before the appearance of the Spanish Armada in the English Channel in 1588.

Sir Francis Drake playing bowls

OPEN VISTAS

At the end of the 1700s, lawns began to gain in importance. On large estates, close-cut grass surrounded the house, sweeping away into the distance, uncluttered by flower beds and trees. The selection of the type of grass started to receive attention. Instead of using hayseed, it was recommended that seed be obtained from grass growing on clean, upland pastures.

USING SCYTHES

Early lawns were cut with a scythe and the trimmings brushed off with a broom; the lawn was then rolled to retain the finely shorn effect that had become popular. In European gardens, early recommendations decreed scything the lawn twice a year, but by the seventeenth century, British lawns were regularly cut twice a month and became much admired.

Budding's lawnmower, 1830

HORSE POWER

Over large areas, lawn rollers were drawn by horses. In 1758, *The Gardener's New Kalendar* recommended: 'The horses should be without shoes and their feet covered with woollen mufflers.'

THE LAWNMOWER COMETH

In 1830 the introduction of the cylinder lawnmower by Edwin Beard Budding (1795–1846) in Britain made it possible to use fine grasses for lawns. Budding's mower was an adaptation of a device that trimmed the pile on cloth, which he had seen when working in a textile factory in Stroud.

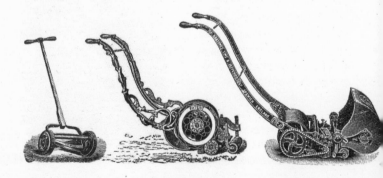

Riding lawnmower, Townsend

POWERED MOWERS

The first gasoline-powered lawnmower appeared about 1900, followed by battery- and mains-powered types. These made it easier – and with less physical effort – to create a finely surfaced and evenly cut lawn. Not withstanding these introductions, in many countries animal-powered lawnmowers remained in use, including bullock-drawn types in Ceylon (now Sri Lanka).

'Moto-Mower' lawnmower, Michigan

CREATING NEW LAWNS

Most new lawns in temperate countries are created by sowing seeds or laying turves (better known as sods in North America). But in warm countries other methods were used, including dibbling (also known as stippling).

DIBBLING

This involved using small clusters of roots, obtained from close-grazed local pasture, dibbled (planted) 5–7.5 cm (2–3 in.) apart into evenly prepared and levelled soil that had been thoroughly watered two or three days earlier and allowed to dry slightly. After completion, the area was lightly rolled and watered; a greensward soon formed.

Summer Afternoon in the Garden, Etching, Christopher Nevinson (1889–1946)

Château Grand Mayne, France

MUD PLASTER!

Another way to create a lawn in a hot climate involved chopping grass roots and stems into pieces 2.5–5 cm (1–2 in.) long. These were mixed with mud to the consistency of mortar and spread evenly over the intended lawn's surface. The entire area needed to be kept lightly moist until a greensward developed.

HA-HA

Fundamentally, a ha-ha is a dry ditch separating a large area of ornamental grass from, usually, pasture used for grazing animals. It enabled a larger vista to be seen without the necessity of obscuring the distant area with a fence. Horace Walpole (1717–97) claimed that the English garden designer Charles Bridgeman (1690–1738) originated the ha-ha, but it was known much earlier in France, appearing at Versailles in the seventeenth century, and was actually introduced into England in about 1695 by the French gardener Monsieur Beaumont.

But why its name? It is said that people in France, when coming across a large, unexpected ditch at the end of a lawn, would gasp 'Ah-ah' or 'Ha-ha'.

TRIMMING LAWN EDGES

The development of well-manicured lawns meant that their edges needed regular trimming. Long-handled edging shears were ideal for use in small areas, but large lawns needed mechanical devices. An advert in the Sydney Mail of June 1881, told of the 'Pall Mall' lawn-edger, which had been patented by Mr. R. Adie, the inventor of the well-known horse-clipper.

Shears were operated by a roller and as it was pushed along a lawn, it cut the lawn's edges quickly, evenly and neatly.

KEEPING PEACOCKS

Peacocks are one of the most ostentatious of creatures, with plumage unparalleled by any other bird. Native to India and Burma, they have been kept on large estates in warm, temperate countries for prestige purposes. And due to the way that the male peacock struts and shows off its plumage, they have become a symbol of pride and vanity.

In Christianity, the peacock is a symbol of eternal life, but in medieval times this did not stop it being eaten by wealthy gentry.

CHAPTER THIRTEEN

Healing Gardens

Natural healing for mind, body and soul has been sought for thousands of years and gardens have played an essential role in improving and maintaining good health through their associated fragrances, shapes, patterns, sounds and, perhaps above all, colours.

COLOUR THERAPY

The range of colours in gardens is wide and many have a healing influence.

❀ Groups of plants with pale blue flowers promote a sense of tranquility, reducing blood pressure, slowing up breathing and lowering the pulse rate.

❀ Buddhists believe deep blue to be the colour of infinity, and often thought it to be the ideal colour for contemplation.

Chinese Buddhist monks

❀ In surveys of favourite colours, blue is usually the most popular and preferred by more than one-third of all people.

❀ White, the colour of purity, creates a sense of coolness and authority.

❀ Yellow is the colour of cheerfulness and is claimed to be the primary colour of hope and productivity.

❀ People who are original in their thoughts prefer yellow.

❀ Green produces a cool and soothing ambience and signifies growth, fertility and freshness. In gardens, shades of green vary, depending on the time of day and the strength of the sun.

PASSIONATE COLOUR

Red is an emotive colour, raising blood pressure and increasing respiration rate. It is also the colour of sexual invitation and this accounts for its ability to raise the pulse rate. Therefore, do not create large splashes of dramatically bright red flowers in a garden that is intended to be an oasis of rest and tranquility.

WHITE AND SILVER GARDENS

With their purity and brightness, white flowers have both a dramatic and a subduing effect. In strong summer sunlight they have an immediate and often penetrating quality, while during the diminishing light of evening they are less forceful but can be seen long after red flowers have faded into the darkness. This makes white especially suitable for a healing garden, where fresh air, restful colours and quiet evening stillness have important recuperative properties.

Galanthus nivalus – snowdrop

Silver is less dominant than white and is usually defined as a lustrous greyish-white or whitish-grey. It reflects light at many angles and this plays an important role in maintaining visual interest.

Herb garden, Venice, 1490

USING BLUE

Traditionally, hospital wards were
painted white or light cream to
reflect cleanliness and purity, but
light blue has increasingly found
favour as a colour to aid recovery.
And these colour themes can be
transferred to gardens.

POSITIONING RED

In India, red symbolizes female
power and all the energy of passion
and positive emotion. In China it is a
lucky colour and is worn by brides.

Dramatic red borders in gardens are
eye-catching throughout the day,
but quickly recede at the onset of
evening. Therefore, always position
plants with less dominantly
coloured flowers at the ends of
borders, as well as at the sides of
garden steps.

YELLOW AND PURPLE

Yellow is a cheerful and optimistic
colour when used in a planting
scheme, but in some early cultures
it was a colour of mourning, for
example for the Egyptians and the
Maya Indians. In Christian Germany
in the fifteenth century, yellow was
said to be offensive to God, and
its complementary colours, violet
and purple, were appropriated

to symbolize mourning and
redemption. In a planting scheme,
a marriage of yellow and purple can
be used to striking effect; consider
the colour of leaves as well as flowers
when planning.

NATURE'S SOUND THERAPY

Sound therapy is popular and its role in healing the mind has been known for thousands of years. Gardens abound in restful sounds, including those of water splashing and tumbling from fountains and waterfalls, and birds with their wide range of territorial and mating calls.

In Japanese gardens, sound is considered to be very important as an aid to contemplation and feelings of serenity. Wind rustling through bamboo leaves, and the hollow, rhythmic notes of the shishi-odoshi (deer-scarer) are used to create areas for meditation. Additionally, the sound of feet walking on gravel and pebbles has a healing quality, reinforcing the need to create a sense of harmony with nature. Essentially, the garden needs to have sounds that are nearby, and those thought to come from a distance.

WIND CHIMES

In Asia, as well as in Mediterranean areas, wind chimes were used to attract benevolent spirits. Chimes remain popular and the sound vibrations are thought to reduce anger and tension.

Woodcut, Julius John Lankes
(1884–1960)

CRUNCHY LEAVES

Deciduous trees have for
centuries been loved for
their autumn leaves which,
when trodden upon, create a
reassuring crunching noise. An
autumnal walk through woods
has long been appreciated as
a way of relaxing and clearing
the mind.

CHINESE WISDOM

Shapes and patterns are claimed
to have a marked influence on our
lives, helping to cure diseases and
to alleviate psychological problems.
Feng shui is an ancient Chinese
version of geomancy and uses the
'cosmic breath' or 'vital spirit' that
runs through the Earth to influence
the fortunes of people. In a garden,
gentle curves that follow the natural
landscape are preferred to straight
lines, which are claimed to give easy
travel to evil spirits.

CHINESE GARDENS

To prevent evil spirits from entering
a garden, the Chinese used screens
(known as 'spirit walls') to face
entrances in outside walls. These
'walls' also ensured greater visual
privacy in gardens. A winding wall

inside a garden was believed to concentrate good luck.

Old and contorted trees were invaluable for attracting and harbouring the cosmic breath. Water also acted as a reservoir for good fortune and was considered especially effective when several small ponds flowed into a larger one.

FOCAL POINTS

For centuries it has been known that attracting the eye to something at the end of a garden helps to diminish introspection and to create a feeling of openness and looking to the future. Plants, statues and buildings all play a part in this philosophy.

TEA CEREMONY GARDENS

The origins of the tea ceremony stretch back to the Chinese monks who drank tea before meditating. In fifteenth-century Japan it was developed as a ritual for the contemplation of something beautiful and to encourage philosophical discussion. By casting off worldly cares, participants achieved a feeling of serenity and were able to concentrate their thoughts.

In special tea ceremony gardens, trees, shrubs and ferns created a timeless landscape that was not confused with seasonal flowers which, by their ephemeral nature, are a continuing reminder of the changing seasons.

HEALING FRAGRANCES

Scent is an unseen power that strongly influences lives and is usually driven by personal preferences. However, scent imprinting was an early part of some religions, creating an atmosphere of rest and spiritual awareness.

Cedrus libani – cedar of Lebanon

❧ The Egyptians believed cedar wood to be imperishable and able to preserve any one enclosed in it. Additionally, cedar oil was used for embalming and the wood burned as incense, an offering to the gods. They also believed their prayers would more rapidly ascend to heaven when mixed with incense smoke.

❧ The Koran, the holy scripture for Muslims and a supreme classic

Magnolia

of Arabic literature, describes Paradise as being filled with nymphs created out of musk. Indeed, the followers of the Prophet Muhammad were so fond of musk that it was frequently mixed with mortar when constructing places of worship.

✤ In China, the now world-renowned philosopher Confucius (551–479 BC), also a teacher and politician, wrote that temples were

hung with blossoms of magnolia, peach, jasmine and jonquil, while incense was burned in homes as well as temples.

The burning of incense was adopted by the Christian faith and has become part of Roman Catholic and High Church religious services.

AROMATHERAPY

The Ancient Egyptians were among the earliest people to show an interest in perfumes and became masters of perfumery; they began importing fragrant plants some 4,000 years ago.

❧ Greeks and Romans took up the use of fragrant oils, although Julius Caesar (100–44 BC) forbade their use as he believed them too effeminate. However, Caligula (AD 12–41), another Roman emperor, embraced them with enthusiasm.

❧ The ever expanding Roman Empire popularized the use of fragrant oils, while Crusaders returning to Europe from Palestine in the eleventh, twelfth and thirteenth centuries added to this knowledge.

❧ During the sixteenth and seventeenth centuries, botanists classified plants according to their healing powers and, by the early part of the 1700s, thirteen essential oils were listed for use in medicine. Unfortunately, as scientific research developed, research into plants as herbal cures diminished. Some old herbal remedies have made a comeback in recent decades and are now highly popular.

a scar. Gattefossé is credited with coining the word 'aromatherapy' to describe his discovery.

❧ As a result of Gattefossé's experiments, Dr Jean Valet successfully used essential oils to treat soldiers injured during the Second World War (1939–45).

❧ In the early 1900s, the French chemist Rene-Maurice Gattefossé burned his hand accidentally and then plunged it in an essential oil extracted from the lavender plant. His hand soon healed without leaving

Lavandula – lavender

❧ By the early 1980s, aromatherapy had become established as a major alternative healing process in much of the world.

Iris 'Florentina' – orris root

ORRIS ROOT

Earlier known as *Iris florentina* and *Iris germanica florentina* and now as *Iris* 'Florentina', orris root has been used in toilet preparations for 2,000 years. The violet-scented roots were lifted, cleaned, dried and ground into preparations such as tooth powder. It is now mainly used as a fixative in perfumery, as well as being an ingredient in potpourri and many brands of gin.

Medicinally, the juice of this plant was used to treat dropsy, and in the dry state was said to be good for lung complaints.

COMFITS

During the fifteenth and sixteenth centuries, confect or comfit boxes were popular. These held a range of sugary pastilles made from seeds, nuts, berries, spices and herbs mixed with honey and saffron. Perhaps such boxes were the equivalent of a medicine chest.

Crocus sativus –
saffron crocus

Pimpinella
anisum –
aniseed

❧ William Shakespeare (1564–1616) knew comfits as 'kissing comforts', as one of their roles was to ensure teeth were clean and the mouth free from bad breath. They were also claimed to 'settle the stomach'. By Regency times (1811–20), the sweets were simply known as comfits.

Myristica fragrans – nutmeg

❧ Comfits were sometimes sold in twists of paper, but to create an impact, ornate comfit boxes were available. Some were carved of wood; others were made of gold or silver and embellished with precious stones and gems.

❧ The usual ingredients of these sugary pills included almonds, anise, caraway, cinnamon, cloves, coriander, fennel, ginger, nutmeg and pepper.

❧ Orris root, dried and ground and combined with gum arabic and sugar, formed firm pastilles and, together with others made from peppermint and ginger, these were also included in comfit boxes.

Lid from a comfit box, Germany, sixteenth century

INDEX